The Coming of Jesus

Gayle Carlton Felton

ABINGDON PRESS
Nashville

THE COMING OF JESUS

by Gayle Carlton Felton

ISBN 0-687-09065-2

00 01 02 03 04 05 06 07 08 09—10 9 8 7 6 5 4 3 2 1

MANUFACTURED IN THE UNITED STATES OF AMERICA

ABINGDON PRESS
Nashville

Contents

Gayle Carlton Felton is an assistant professor of Christian Nurture at Duke Divinity School. She is a clergy member of the North Carolina Annual Conference and was a member of the Baptismal Study Committee that developed *By Water and the Spirit: A United Methodist Understanding of Baptism*. She is also the author of *This Gift of Water* (Abingdon, 1992).

A Word of Welcome

Welcome to *The Coming of Jesus*, a study of the events leading up to the birth of Jesus Christ and of his early years. Jesus' early years are one of the mysteries of our faith. What was his life like? What did he do during these "lost years" from infancy to puberty and from his date with the Temple leaders at age twelve until his baptism as an adult? Perhaps we will never know.

Much that we can know is contained in these pages. Here you will find

- an introduction to the infancy narratives in the Gospel of Matthew and the Gospel of Luke and an exploration of how these events fulfilled the prophecies for the Messiah;
- background information about Jesus' culture and history as a faithful Jew in the heritage of Abraham, Isaac, and Jacob and of the social and religious institutions of which he was a part;
- a historical perspective of the conflict of kingdoms that Jesus' birth set in motion;
- an introduction to the key figures in the prelude and postlude to Jesus' birth: Zechariah, Elizabeth, Joseph, Mary, Simeon, Anna, the shepherds, the wise men, and the angels;
- excerpts from noncanonical birth narratives that are not considered part of our Scripture but that provide some tantalizing clues to the traditions we hold about Jesus, Mary, and Joseph. It must be emphasized that these selections are *not* offered as Scripture but as examples of early writing circulated in the Christian community about the life of Jesus.

We invite you to delve deeply into this study of Jesus' early life and of his roots and pray that you will find a blessing in it.

How to Use This Resource

We hope you enjoy participating in this study, either on your own or with a group. We offer these hints and suggestions to make your study a success.

The Coming of Jesus is a self-contained study with all the teaching/learning suggestions conveniently located on or near the main text to which they refer. They are identified with the same heading (or a close abbreviation) as those in the main text. In addition to your Bible, this book provides all you need to have a successful group or individual study session.

There are some special features as well, such as the **Bible 301** activities in the teaching helps. We usually think of the "101" designation as the beginning study level; these "301" designations prompt you to dig deeper. In these sections, you are invited to look up Scriptures, key words, or concepts in a Bible dictionary, commentary, or atlas. On occasion, an added book or resource is cited that may be obtained from your local library or perhaps from your pastor. These resources are extras; your study will be enriched by these added sources of information, but it is not dependent on them.

This study is intentionally invitational. In the closing activity, you are invited to do three things: to give prayerful consideration to your relationship to Jesus Christ and make or renew your commitment, to offer your own spoken prayers, and to pray with and for others. We trust you will participate in these activities as you feel comfortable and that you will use them as a challenge to grow more confident in prayer and with your covenant with Jesus Christ.

Session One

The Events Have Been Fulfilled Among Us

Session Focus ■

In order to understand and appreciate the biblical accounts of the coming of Jesus, some basic information and ideas need to be introduced. This session focuses on the concepts, terminology, and interpretive approaches that will undergird all of the sessions.

Session Objective ■

The "Christmas story" is so familiar to most Christians that it may have lost its impact on our minds and hearts. Our objective is to hear again the good news of the coming of Christ and to experience anew the transforming power of this mighty act of God.

Session Preparation ■

Read chapters one and two in the Gospels of Matthew and Luke. Try to read as if you had never heard these stories before. Using a less familiar version of the Bible might help. Then read Mark 1 and John 1 noting how differently from Matthew and Luke these writers begin their stories about Christ.

In tiny St. Mary's Episcopal Church near Glendale Springs, North Carolina, there is an unusual fresco. Done by painter Ben Long in 1974, *Mary Great with Child* is said to be one of very few artistic renderings of the pregnant Mary, mother of Jesus. The painting projects a palatable sense of expectant waiting; the birth is soon to be. Painted above Mary's head is an eclipse of the sun. Although almost totally covered by the moon, rays of sunlight are visible around the sphere. The world waits in darkness for the imminent coming of the Christ. Even in darkness, the divine light cannot be completely obscured.

The theme of light coming into the darkness appears in many places in the Bible as a metaphor of God's grace breaking through to offer hope and joy to those trapped in the gloom of sin. Indeed, the biblical story opens with the creation of light (see Genesis 1:3-4). In Isaiah 9:2, often understood as a prophecy of the coming of the Messiah, we read, "The people who walked in darkness / have seen a great light; / those who lived in a land of deep darkness / on them light has shined." A later prophecy proclaims, "Arise, shine; for your light has come, / and the glory of the LORD has risen upon you. / For darkness

Events Fulfilled ■

The theme of light and darkness is not as powerful for us as it was for people living in Bible times. Today, it is often difficult to get far enough from city lights to have a clear view of the nighttime sky. Then, the darkness was broken only by lamps, candles, and fires. Perhaps you have visited a cave or underground cavern and experienced the utter, intense darkness. Exodus 10:21 describes the plague of darkness on the Egyptians as "a darkness that can be felt."

Use these thoughts and the several Scripture references to light in order to describe and consider the potency of the theme of darkness and light. How does this image work for you? What does it say to you?

What does it suggest to you that the time chosen to observe Christmas was based on the time of winter solstice in the Northern Hemisphere?

How is the celebration of Jesus' birth "light" to you?

The Old Testament ■

Read the following passages in Matthew and the

shall cover the earth, / and thick darkness the peoples; / but the LORD will arise upon you, / and his glory will appear over you" (Isaiah 60:1-2).

In the New Testament this metaphor is a favorite of John's, as evidenced in the beautiful prologue to his Gospel, "The light shines in the darkness, and the darkness did not overcome it. . . . The true light, which enlightens everyone, was coming into the world" (1:5, 9). Finally, in the closing vision of the Holy City of God in Revelation 22:5, the saints are assured: "And there will be no more night; they need no light of lamp or sun, for the Lord God will be their light, and they will reign forever and ever." Taking notice of this theme of light is an appropriate way to launch our study of the coming of Jesus Christ into the world.

As early as the fourth century, the church came to celebrate the birth of Christ at a time that, in their society, was associated with light. The winter solstice marks the point when there is the least light—the shortest day of the year. But, it is also the beginning of the gradual but certain lengthening of the day, as light again triumphs over darkness. Many non-Christian religious groups in the early centuries, especially those that venerated the sun, held elaborate festivals to observe the solstice. The same season, specifically December 25, became the time when Christians celebrated the coming of the true light: "Again Jesus spoke to them, saying, 'I am the light of the world. Whoever follows me will never walk in darkness but will have the light of life' " (John 8:12).

The Old Testament (Hebrew Bible)

The Christian church from its beginning has often struggled with the Old

Old Testament passages given in parentheses to which they refer: **Matthew 1:22-23** (Isaiah 7:14); **2:5-6** (Micah 5:2 and 2 Samuel 5:2); **2:14-15** (Exodus 4:22-23 and Deuteronomy 1:31); **2:16-18** (Exodus 1:15-22); **2:21-23** (Isaiah 11:1 and Zechariah 3:6 and 6:12).

What do you think is Matthew's purpose in grounding these events in the Hebrew Scriptures?

The Infancy Narratives ■

Both Judaism and Christianity are historical religions, believing that God reveals the divine self through events of a linear history, beginning with God's act of Creation and moving toward a climax in which God's purpose will be fully realized. Why is the linear understanding of history so significant in Christianity?

Read Matthew 1–2 and Luke 1–2. On a piece of poster paper, indicate two columns, one for Matthew and one for Luke. List the preparatory events each mentions. (More attention is given these chapters and this "Matthew–Luke chart" later in the session.)

Testament—how much value it has for Christians and how Christians should use it. Even today, most Christians are much more familiar and comfortable with the New Testament. Some Christian leaders have even proposed that the church should use only the New Testament. Matthew and Luke would have been both perplexed and horrified at such an idea. They, and all of the New Testament writers, knew that the Christian faith has its grounding in the story of God's work in the life of the people of Israel. Indeed, understanding and appreciation of almost every New Testament passage, including the infancy narratives of Matthew and Luke, is richly enhanced by knowledge of the Old Testament background and heritage.

The Infancy Narratives

Stories of the birth of Jesus are told only in the Gospels of Matthew and Luke. These accounts are called "the infancy narratives," although they are not strictly limited to Jesus' infancy. The term is applied to all of the material in Matthew and Luke preceding the birth and, in the case of Luke, even an event that occurred when Jesus was twelve. Both writers set the stage for the events of their drama by carefully arranging the background. Jesus' birth is presented as the culmination of a long period of divine preparation, now drawing to its climax. The infancy narratives announce the end of a long period of waiting. Now God is doing a new thing, a wonderful thing. It is only within God's overall plan of history that the coming of Christ can be understood.

Other New Testament Accounts

It is helpful to note that the New Testament account of the life and work of

The New Testament starts with the Gospels, which relate Jesus' life and ministry, but which were written after Paul's letters. What is the most important "starting place" for you in your faith and faith development: the story of Jesus life? his teachings? God's saving act through Jesus' crucifixion and resurrection? Jesus' place in the Godhead? something else?

Jesus Christ developed backwards in time. The letters of Paul, most of which were written before any of the Gospels, show very little interest in events in the earthly life of Jesus. These letters are concerned with the meaning of Christ—how the Christ event is to be understood and what it means in the lives of individuals and in the early Christian communities.

Paul's emphasis is on the resurrected Christ through whom all persons may come into new life through the transforming work of the Holy Spirit. He presents the theological significance of this work of God in Christ and applies its meaning to the ethical lives of Christians. For Paul and the other early New Testament authors, Jesus becomes God's chosen Savior in the event of the Resurrection, when God brought him back from the dead and made him an eternal part of the Godhead.

Even the Synoptic Gospels themselves developed "backwards." The death and resurrection of Christ early on were considered most important. Then more interest developed in his public ministry and still later in his birth.

The Synoptic Gospels

The Synoptic Gospels are Matthew, Mark, and Luke. They are so called because their accounts can, at least partially, be harmonized or brought together. John's Gospel is quite different.

The earliest of the Gospels to be written is that of Mark. While Mark tells much more about the earthly life of Jesus than Paul does, he does not relate any stories about Jesus' birth. Instead Mark opens his Gospel with the ministry of John the Baptist and his baptism of Jesus. Jesus' baptism, at around thirty years of age, is the beginning of his ministry. Through his account of the descent of the Holy Spirit upon Jesus and the voice of God claiming him as God's son, Mark expresses his understanding that is the moment at which Jesus becomes the Christ. This view is sometimes called *adoptionism*—the idea that God "adopted" the person Jesus and designated him to be God's instrument in the establishment of God's reign on the earth.

In contrast, John, the last of the four Gospels to be written, understands Jesus Christ to be the human being in whom the preexistent Word of God (existing as a part of God before Creation) came into the world. In the Gospels of Matthew and Luke, the "Christological moment"—the point at which Jesus the human becomes Christ, God's chosen Messiah—is at his conception in the womb of his mother Mary. This is what these two writers are expressing in their accounts of the virgin birth (better, the virgin conception).

Read Mark 1:1-15 and John 1:1-18. Discuss the "Christological moment" as explained in this section. Chart the understandings by each Gospel writer as to when Jesus became Christ. How does this influence your own thought?

Introduction to Matthew 1–2

On the Matthew–Luke chart, add (or note) elements in each Gospel that are distinctive, even contrary, to each other.

Read Matthew's genealogy (1:1-17). What does it mean that this is not so much a family tree as a summary of Israel's salvation history? Who are the key **men** in this genealogy and what was their role in the unfolding of God's promise of land and blessing? (Start with Abraham in Genesis 12.)

Introduction to Matthew's Infancy Narratives in Chapters 1 and 2

In Matthew's Gospel, the birth of Jesus is the climax of a historical development that began with God's call of Abraham in Genesis 12. Matthew indicates little interest in the actual historical situation in Palestine in the first century. His focus is the ongoing story of God's actions in history. He presents the genealogy of Jesus (1:1-17) not as a human family tree but as a summary of Israel's salvation history.

Matthew purports to divide the period from Abraham to the Messiah into three units of fourteen full generations each (although oddly the last has only thirteen—

Jesus would represent the beginning, not the completion, of the fourteenth generation). The genealogy is structured around the kingship of David—the high point of Israel's national existence. The first unit ends with David's accession to the throne (verse 6). The second unit is concluded when the kingship of David's successors is ended by the conquest and exile into Babylon (verse 11). The third unit climaxes with the birth of Jesus whom Matthew sees as the restoration of Davidic rule. Clearly this genealogy is a theological creation designed to set Jesus in the context of Old Testament history. It is not intended to be a factual family tree; therefore, questions about its differences from the genealogy presented by Luke (3:23-38) are not relevant.

An intriguing aspect of Matthew's genealogy is the unusual inclusion of women. Since descent was traced through the male line, perhaps this is a signal by Matthew that the coming of Jesus will bring about the new and unexpected. Five women are named as part of the family line. All of them are women who acted outside the social rules of their time in order to carry forward God's purpose. The lives of none of these women are in conformity with traditional domestic arrangement of the Old Testament period. Their stories indicate that Matthew recognized that God works in unpredictable ways and through persons who are not in positions of traditional power and influence.

Another interesting aspect of the genealogy is Matthew's tracing of the line of Joseph, "the husband of Mary, of whom Jesus was born" (1:16b). Clearly Matthew considers Joseph to be the legal father of Jesus, if not a biological parent. Joseph's acceptance of Mary as his wife and her child as his son

Using a Bible dictionary, investigate the Old Testament accounts of the four Old Testament women included in Jesus' genealogy in Matthew. Who are they? Read Genesis 38:6-30, Joshua 2, Ruth 3, and 2 Samuel 11. What does it mean that Jesus' genealogy includes women who were Gentile or of questionable repute? What might God be saying to us through their stories?

Then turn to Mary. What do you know about Mary from the Bible? from tradition?

Bible 301 ☐

If you can obtain a copy of The Lost Books of the Bible, *look through The Gospel of the Birth of Mary or through The Protevangelion (also known as the Gospel of James) for accounts of the early life of Mary and of the birth of Jesus. What traditions do we have of Mary and Joseph that derive from these nonbiblical birth narratives?*

Introduction to ■ Luke 1–2

As we study Luke's Gospel, we must remind ourselves that we too are Gentiles. How might this realization help us to hear Luke's message better?

Read the genealogy (Luke 3:23-38). Note the differences between this genealogy and Matthew's. Note them on the Matthew–Luke chart. What message does Luke seem to want to convey?

establishes him as the adoptive father. Therefore, it is essential for Matthew's purpose of portraying Jesus as a descendant of King David for Joseph to be in the line of Davidic descent.

In the two chapters that make up Matthew's infancy narrative, certain themes can be recognized. One is the pervasive presentation of Jesus as the fulfillment of God's work in the history of Israel in the past. Another is the reality that it is the action of God that determines events, even when the divine presence is not apparent to the humans involved. Indeed, God works through ordinary people, even including women and Gentiles. Third, Matthew clearly portrays Jesus as the royal Messiah, the son of David, Israel's great king. All of these themes will be developed more fully.

Luke 1–2: The Infancy Narrative

The infancy stories in Luke occupy almost twice as much space as those in Matthew and in many ways are very different. There is no evidence that the two writers drew from a common source. We understand neither narrative as completely factual. The writers' purpose was not so much to report as to interpret. Luke was almost surely a Gentile convert to Christianity. He attempts to understand Judaism and Christianity from that standpoint rather than from the Jewish perspective of Matthew.

Writing for Gentile readers primarily, Luke insists in his Gospel (as well as in Acts, his second volume) that salvation through Christ was intended for both Jews and Gentiles. From the beginning, the inclusion of Gentiles was a part of the divine plan.

Much more than Matthew, Luke is concerned to set his account within the larger story of history, not just that of the Jews. His genealogy of Jesus in chapter 3 traces back to Adam—the father of all humankind—rather than to Abraham through whom God brought the Hebrew people into being. In the infancy narrative, he seeks to relate the events surrounding the birth of Jesus to concrete historical circumstances in the context of the Greco-Roman world of the first century.

Luke's infancy narrative easily divides into seven episodes. First, there is the annunciation of the coming birth of the child who will grow up to be known as John the Baptist. This announcement is made first to the child's father Zechariah. Second is the annunciation to Mary of the conception and birth of a son to be named Jesus. Both annunciations are by God's messenger, the angel Gabriel. Third is Mary's visitation to the home of Elizabeth. The fourth episode includes the birth, circumcision, naming, and prophecy of Elizabeth and Zechariah's son. The fifth is the birth of Jesus and the visitation of the angels and shepherds. Next is the scene of the presentation of Jesus in the Temple where Simeon and Anna see him. The final event of the infancy narrative is his parents' finding the twelve-year-old Jesus in conversation with Jewish leaders in the Temple. This last episode is the only glimpse of Jesus that the New Testament offers in the time between his infancy and his adulthood.

Luke recognizes that if his Gentile Christian community is to grasp the significance of the coming of Christ, it must also understand the history of Israel specifically. In the first two chapters he makes the transition from the story of Israel to the story of Jesus. The infancy narratives function as a bridge connecting God's work in the history

Form seven teams or assign to seven individuals these different movements of Luke's infancy narrative: Luke 1:5-25; 1:26-38; 1:39-56; 1:57-80; 2:1-20; 2:21-40; 2:41-52.

What happens in this segment of Scripture? What do we learn about the context of Jesus early life? about the religious laws and practices of the Hebrews? about the civil authorities and life under Roman rule? about how God works through persons in both predictable and in extraordinary ways? What reversals or surprises are there?

of the Jews to God's new work in and through Jesus Christ. The characters of these narratives are very much like those of the Old Testament. Many of the events are related in patterns common to the record of Hebrew salvation history.

How do these stories serve as a "bridge between the testaments"? (Recall Matthew's heavy use of the device, "This took place to fulfill what had been spoken by the Lord through the prophet"). How does Luke hearken to themes and promises from the Hebrew Scriptures? How often does Luke have one of these major figures refer to the image of righteousness, salvation, restoration, or redemption?

While both Matthew and Luke lean heavily upon the story of God's action in the history of Israel, they use the Old Testament differently. Matthew uses numerous specific quotations, especially from the Prophetic Literature. He does not claim that the writers or speakers of this material in its original settings necessarily intended to prophesy about the Messiah. As a Christian though, he applies these quotations directly to events around the birth of Jesus to make the point that Jesus truly is the fulfillment of these prophecies.

Luke uses fewer Old Testament quotations, preferring to allude to persons and events in ways that make connections to Jesus. Both writers are intent on establishing the close relationship between the Old Testament story and the story of Jesus Christ. This is one indication of the high significance of these rather brief accounts in the first two chapters of these two Gospels. In the words of distinguished scholar Raymond Brown, writing in *The Birth of the Messiah*, (Doubleday, 1979), "For both evangelists the infancy narrative is the place where the OT and the Gospel most directly meet."

Dating the Birth of Jesus

Dating the Birth of Jesus

What does the Bible say about the actual date of Jesus' birth?

What are your thoughts about the contemporary

Dating the Birth of Jesus Christ

In studying the coming of Jesus, especially in Luke's Gospel, one encounters what appears to be confusion, even contradiction, about his birth date. Most scholars contend that Jesus was probably born between 6 and 4 B.C. How can it be that Jesus was born "Before Christ"?

What is the relative impor- tance of using globally a dating system initially based on Christianity rather than on an older religious tradition or some secular marker (such as the years since the founding of Rome)?

American Christians are so familiar with the division of human history into B.C. and A.D. that we seldom give it much considera- tion. The date 2000 signifies that it has been 2,000 years since the birth of Christ. Only in official ceremonial proclamations and other such formal situations do we see A.D. added to the number of the year. It is simply assumed, on the same principle by which any number written without a minus sign in front of it is recognized as a positive number. So, most of the Western world uses a dating system that divides history into a period before Christ (B.C.) and a still-continuing period of years designated as "the years of our Lord," the English translation of the Latin phrase *Anno Domini* (A.D.) Numbers of years in the B.C. period become smaller as they approach the time of Christ, like nega- tive numbers on a number scale.

For many centuries, the typical method of dating was to reckon years since the found- ing of Rome. But in the sixth century A.D., Pope John I supposedly commissioned a Syrian monk named Dionysius Exiguus (Dennis the Short, in English) to come up with a system for determining the date of Easter. As a part of his work, Dionysius changed the scheme of numbering years to one based upon the birth of Christ. He determined that Christ had been born 753 years after the founding of Rome, thus the Roman year 754 became the Christian year A.D. 1. By the fourteenth century, this method of dating was in general use.

The Common Era ■

As an exercise in imagina- tion, suppose that a neutral global dating methodology were to be instituted that was based on an event or

The "Common Era"

The designations B.C.E. meaning "Before the Common Era" and C.E. meaning the "Common Era" are sometimes used in place of the traditional designations that refer to

system common to all people, regardless of religion, nationality, and so on. What event or common system might be used? (Don't become stymied by how hard it might be to implement; just assume it could be possible.) What might that kind of inclusive methodology mean to the potential unity of our world nations?

Christ. The common factor is the global usage of this dating convention. This is 2000 or 2004, for example, all over the world, even though many different traditions have their own calendars. Although the time periods are the same, "Common Era" is understood as a global reckoning, not a religious one.

The problem was that Dionysius unfortunately made an error in his calculation of the year of Christ's birth. From other historical sources we know that King Herod died in 4 B.C.; both Matthew and Luke say that Jesus was born during Herod's reign. So the result of a human mistake in calculation is that Jesus was born a few years before what we now know as the B.C.–A.D. division. This is of little real consequence and has nothing to do with the accuracy or intent of biblical material, but it can be a cause of perplexity if not understood.

The Conflated Creche ■

Think about the Nativity pageants you have seen or participated in or examine a Nativity set or manger scene noting the various participants. What are the values of conflating the Matthew and Luke stories? What are the dangers?

Keep in mind as the Gospel writers tell their stories that they heavily compress history and narrative. Read Matthew 2:1 and 16; the wise men could have visited perhaps two years after the birth, yet the flow of the story makes it seem more imme-

The Conflated Creche

Another potential point of confusion is the "conflated creche." The traditional Nativity scenes in our churches and homes during Advent, Christmas, and sometimes Epiphany are tangible proof of how we often read the Bible. A quick check of the infancy narratives in Matthew and Luke reveals that the Matthean magi and the Lucan shepherds are not a part of the same story. While the shepherds visited the Christ Child on the night of his birth, the wise men came later and visited the Holy Family in their house. Matthew knew no shepherds; Luke knew no magi.

The point is not that we should change our Nativity scenes. It is rather that this confusion is evidence that too often we read biblical material with fixed preconceptions of what it is going to say, instead of opening

diate. How do you keep a sense of perspective about what happened as you read and interpret the Gospel story?

our hearts and minds to apprehend and comprehend what it *does* say. This traditional conflation, or merging of stories and characters around the manger, is a signal that we must again and again remind ourselves to listen and to learn anew.

Closing Prayer

Consider using a circle prayer during your study in which all participants can offer a prayer of petition, thanks, or concern, for example, in turn.

The theme of Christ's coming invites you to consider your own commitment and relationship to Jesus Christ. Take time in your prayer to make or reaffirm that commitment.

Close with a circle prayer that includes prayers for those who do not know Jesus Christ and the light that he brings to the world.

Session Two

Jesus Was a Jew

Session Focus ■

Most of us think of Jesus as a Christian rather than a Jew. But, of course, the man Jesus was Jewish and cannot be understood apart from that religious and cultural background. This session will enable us not only to know Judaism better but also to know Jesus better.

Session Objective ■

The history of the Hebrew people as presented in the Old Testament spans many centuries and can be confusing. This session will briefly summarize that salvation history and outline it chronologically. The session also will consider significant Jewish beliefs and practices that characterized Jesus' community. In addition, this session will seek to engender a more developed appreciation for Judaism in its own right and as the "parent of Christianity."

Session Preparation ■

Visit a synagogue or talk with a rabbi in order to get a "flavor" of this great faith. Talk to Jewish co-workers and friends about their beliefs and practices. Look

Robert A. Spivey and D. Moody Smith begin their widely used textbook on the New Testament with this paragraph:

Jesus was a Jew. So were his first disciples. *Jesus Christ* means Jesus the Messiah of Israel, the anointed king of Davidic lineage (cf. 2 Sam. 7:12-15 and Psalm 89:3-4). In fact, the earliest Christians did not think of themselves as members of a new religion separate from Judaism. Yet Jesus and his disciples represented something new within Judaism. This newness consisted not in original or unique ideas but in the aspects of ancient traditions and hopes that were taken up, reinterpreted, and emphasized (*Anatomy of the New Testament*: Prentice Hall, 1969, 1995).

It is impossible to comprehend the meaning of the coming of Jesus Christ without knowing something about first-century Judaism. For many years, Christian scholars knew little about the beliefs and practices of first-century Jews. Educated guesses and theories were based on Jewish sources that were written centuries later. A great deal of recent scholarship has been devoted to the study of Judaism at the time of Jesus. The discovery and use of ancient documents that provide more information and insight have aided this effort. These documents include the Dead

at a calendar that indicates both Jewish and Christian holidays and compare the times of the year at which they are celebrated. Browse a greeting card shop to see how many cards you can find that celebrate Jewish festivals.

Choose from among these activities and discussion starters to plan your lesson.

Jesus Was a Jew

Do you think of Jesus as a Jew or as a Christian? Does thinking about Jesus as a Jew have any impact on your Christian beliefs? Explain.

Ask group members what they know about Jewish festivals and customs. Update your information as the session progresses.

A People in Covenant

Read through the Scripture references in Genesis to get a sense of the movement of the story.

Discuss the meaning of *covenant*—a basic concept in both Testaments. Circumcision was the sign of the old covenant between God and the Hebrew people through the men. Christians understand that baptism is the sign of the new covenant between God and the Christian church. The other Christian sacrament—Holy Communion—is also related to the covenant between

Sea Scrolls, the Pseudepigrapha, and works of Jewish Hellenistic authors.

Archaeological discoveries, such as ancient inscriptions and the ruins of synagogues also continue to expand our comprehension. It has become clear that first-century Judaism was not a religion with uniform beliefs and practices that were imposed upon all Jews as orthodoxy. Instead, it was an alive and growing faith within which much diversity was accepted and allowed to flourish.

The Pseudepigrapha

The books that make up the Pseudepigrapha are Jewish and Jewish-Christian religious works written between 200 B.C.. and A.D. 200. These writings are outside of the canon of both Jews and Christians, but contribute significantly to our understanding of religious thought in the intertestamental period.

A People in Covenant With God

Judaism, as Christianity, is a historical religion. God reveals the divine self to human beings through the events of history. The first five books of the Hebrew Bible (Old Testament) are especially important as the record of God's actions in the early centuries. Called the Pentateuch or Torah, these books contain a mixture of historical facts and legendary tales that together unfold the story of God's acts and the Hebrew people's response.

The Jewish people trace their origins back to Abraham, who was called by God and sent into the land of Palestine, which God promised to give to him and his descendants. God established a covenant with Abraham (then called Abram), promising to make him and his wife Sarah parents of a people

God and the Christian church. Blood was a token of covenants throughout the Old Testament. The blood at circumcision and the blood of sacrificial animals are perhaps the best examples. Read Genesis 17 and 1 Corinthians 11:23-25. Are there any common elements to these covenant announcements? What does it mean when we use Jesus' words in our celebrations of Holy Communion?

through whom God would work to bring salvation to all persons (Genesis 12, 15). The human side of this covenant relationship was the responsibility to be obedient to God's will. The sign of God's covenant is the circumcision of every Jewish male (Genesis 17). The covenant promise was renewed to Abraham and Sarah's son Isaac (26:23-25), and then to Isaac and Rebekah's son Jacob (28:10-17). Through his wives Leah and Rachel and his concubines, Jacob (later called Israel) was the father of twelve sons.

These "patriarchs" are seen as the progenitors of the twelve tribes that made up the Hebrew people, often called the "children of Israel." Jacob's favorite son was Joseph whom he lavished with gifts and privileges. Resentful of this favoritism and Joseph's attitude of superiority, his brothers sold him into slavery in Egypt (37:12-28). There his ability to interpret dreams eventually made him a favorite of Pharaoh, and he became the chief administrator in the Egyptian government (41:37-49). When his brothers were forced to come to buy food during a time of famine, Joseph forgave them and brought the entire family to live in Egypt (46:1-7).

A People of the Exodus

Form seven teams to look over the main movements of the Exodus event: Exodus 1–2 (the enslavement); 3–4 (call of Moses); 5–6 (oppression worsens); 7–8 (four plagues); 9–10 (five more plagues); 11–12 (the last plague); 13–14 (the escape).

What happens in each of these movements? How does God interact with the

A People of the Exodus

Centuries later, the Hebrew people descended from Joseph; and his brothers had grown numerous. Under a different governing authority in Egypt, their status had changed radically. Rather than guests, they had become slaves to the Egyptians. They were cruelly burdened with labor on the Pharaoh's massive building projects. In spite of the Hebrew's status as slaves, the Egyptians feared the Hebrews and felt threatened by their growing numbers. Finally Pharaoh ordered the killing of all

people? with Moses? with Pharaoh? What does this event mean to your faith?

This is the central saving event of the Hebrew Scriptures; Jesus' death and resurrection is the central saving event of the New Testament. What would this salvation history mean to Jesus? How might Jesus' knowledge of this salvation history have prepared him for his role as Messiah?

Using a Bible dictionary, look up *first-born* to get an idea of the importance of the first-born son or male animal to the Hebrews. In many cultures, special family responsibilities and expectations were placed on the eldest son. What import would this final plague have had on the Hebrews?

Quickly review Exodus 20:1-17. These commandments made up the essence of the law that Jesus learned and said he came to fulfill. In what ways did he fulfill these laws? What do these laws mean to you today? Do you observe them?

Bible 301 ☐

Read carefully Exodus 12 and 13, which describe the observance of the Passover.

Hebrew male infants (Exodus 1). Exodus 2:23-25 says that the people cried out to God, and "God heard their groaning, and God remembered his covenant with Abraham, Isaac, and Jacob."

Continuing to act in their history, God called Moses to the task of leading the Hebrew people out of their bondage. After difficult and prolonged negotiations, the Israelites fled Egypt with Moses in command. In a mighty way, God acted to deliver them by parting the waters of the sea to enable them to escape Pharaoh's pursuit (Exodus 3–15).

This pivotal occurrence in Hebrew history, known as the Exodus, is still commemorated annually at the Festival of Passover. It is considered the formative, creative event of Jewish history—the time when God made Israel a nation. The name recalls God's protection of the Hebrews from the plagues sent upon Egypt to persuade Pharaoh to release the captives. The final plague was the death of the firstborn son of every Egyptian family and flock. The Hebrews were warned by God to mark the doorposts of their dwellings with the blood of lambs. When the angel of death came, he "passed over" the marked homes.

For years, the freed people lived in the desert wilderness under the leadership of Moses. God provided for their sustenance by sending manna and quail (see Exodus 16 and Numbers 11:16-35). It was during this period that God gave them a clearer, more comprehensive revelation of their side of the covenant. Covenants always involve both promises and responsibilities on both sides. On Mount Sinai, the law (Torah) was given by God to Moses to teach all of the people (Exodus 20:1-17). Epitomized in the Ten Commandments, the law is delineated in

Explore the Seder meal to
learn about the symbolic
foods and actions of
Passover observance as well
as the ritual retelling of the
story of Israel's deliverance.
If possible, get help from a
host synagogue or rabbi.

Monarchy, Conquest, and Exile ■

Construct a timeline,
preferably on newsprint or
butcher paper, of the major
events of Old Testament
history. **You will be asked
to update this timeline in
future sessions, so post it
in an accessible place.**
Precise dates are not
important; indeed, many of
them are unknown. The
purpose is to comprehend
the overall chronology of
some of the significant
events and people.

The monarchy was really a
theocracy: a nation ruled
by God through a temporal
leader. If the nation were
conquered, in a real sense
to the people, God had also
been conquered. Imagine
what our nation (without
being a theocracy) would
be like if the President,
Congress, scientists, engi-
neers, computer profes-
sionals, business persons,

detail in Exodus, Leviticus, Numbers, and
Deuteronomy. Moses' successor was Joshua
who, obeying God's command, led the
Israelites in the conquest and settlement of
the land that God had first promised to
Abraham—variously called Canaan,
Palestine, or the Holy Land.

Monarchy, Conquest, and Exile

The people of Israel formed a confederacy
of the twelve tribes and were for about two
centuries led by "judges." These judges were
not limited to juridical duties. They were
men and women whom God raised up and
empowered to unify the tribes, especially in
times of warfare. Deborah, Gideon, and
Samson are the best-remembered judges.

Approximately ten centuries before the time
of Christ, the nation of Israel became a
monarchy with the king understood to be chosen by God. Samuel, who might be called the
last of the judges and the first of the prophets,
anointed the first two kings, Saul (1020–1000)
and David (1005–961). During their reigns
there was an almost constant struggle against a
neighboring people, the Philistines.

This conflict is most familiar to us in the
story of the boy David slaying the giant
Goliath (1 Samuel 17). The great King David
and his son Solomon took the nation to its
pinnacle of size, wealth, and power. Never
before or after would Israel enjoy such a position of prominence. A grand Temple was
built to replace the Tabernacle that had been
the main center of worship earlier. It was
richly decorated and luxuriously equipped. It
became the site of the Jewish system of worship based upon the use of animal sacrifices.
After Solomon's reign (961–928), the kingdom split forming the nations of Israel in the
north and Judah in the south.

artists, musicians, teachers, clergy, doctors, and health-care professionals were all sent into exile. How would we function? Who would rise up to lead (if allowed to do so)? What would the "average" citizen do? What kind of religious crisis, if any, would this precipitate?

What shape might our religious services take, if we were allowed to have them? Who would lead? How might this oppression shape your perception of God? of worship? of your faith? Would you feel abandoned by God (as the Hebrews frequently did)? that this crisis came about because of our national sinfulness (as the Hebrews thought)? that God was not strong enough or did not care enough about us to save us (as the Hebrews feared)? Explain.

The kingdom of Israel with its capital at Samaria was made up of ten of the tribes. In 721, it was conquered by the Assyrian Empire and the people taken into an exile from which they never returned. The name *Israel*, however, continued to be used.

The kingdom of Judah with its capital at Jerusalem was ruled by kings in the dynasty of David. It was conquered by the Babylonian Empire in the sixth century B.C. and much of its population taken into captivity in two major deportations in 597 and 587. After several decades, the remnants of the people of Judah (the origin of the term *Jews*) were allowed by their Persian overlords to return to their land (around 539). It was in this period of exile and return that the Jewish people came to understand themselves as "people of the Book." They believed that God had provided all that was needed in their Holy Scriptures—the Law, the Prophets, and the Writings.

The centuries just summarized were the period of the prophets, beginning with men such as Nathan, Elijah, and Elisha and continuing with "the writing prophets" whose books make up a large part of the Hebrew Bible. The Hebrew prophets should not be thought of primarily as predictors of the future. They were pre-eminently spokespersons for God; their proclamations were usually introduced with the phrase, "thus says the LORD."

The Old Testament ends roughly at the time of Alexander the Great who, by 323, had conquered the Persian Empire and most of the known world. The story of the successor kingdoms into which his empire was divided, the Maccabean War for Jewish independence, the Hasmonean dynasty, and the Roman conquest will be related in session 3.

The Temple

Add to your timeline the construction and destruction of the three Temples in Jewish history. Look in your study Bible or a Bible dictionary for diagrams of the Temple.

What was the importance of the Temple to the Israelites? Why do you think so many areas of the Temple were segregated?

Exodus 25–29 has elaborate descriptions and instructions for the Tabernacle, the priests, and their garments. Read these chapters. What was the Tabernacle like? What was it for? Who presided?

Now look at 1 Kings 5–8 for information on the building of the first Temple by Solomon. (Ezekiel 40–44 is the prophet's vision of a restored Temple and priesthood, but Ezra 3–6 reports on the actual building of the second Temple.) How do the Temples compare?

The Temple

By the time that Jesus was born, the third Temple had been largely completed. With its huge stones, it was one of the amazing feats of ancient building. Built on the same site as the tenth-century Temple of Solomon and the second Temple, constructed after the return from Exile (520–515), this Temple was magnificent. Herod the Great had begun the rebuilding in 20 to 19 B.C. Within a year and a half, the main building was erected. The forecourts and enclosures required another eight years. Finishing work on the Temple continued long after Herod's death. Indeed, it was not all done until just a few years before its destruction by the Romans in A.D. 70. Like its predecessors, it had three parts. There was a porch with steps; the sanctuary or holy place, which was the main room; and the small Holy of Holies.

Outside the Temple was a series of courts. Outermost was a large Court of the Gentiles with its porches of colonnades. Its area was larger than the hilltop on which the Temple was built. A retaining wall had to be constructed and fill dirt brought in. A part of this wall is the only surviving portion of the Temple today. The western part is the famous Wailing Wall, where Jews and many Christians from all over the world come to pray.

The Court of the Gentiles was the place where animals were sold for sacrifice and money was changed from the Roman coin to special currency acceptable for giving in the Temple. It was also the only area open to non-Jews. Its interior walls displayed inscriptions in Hebrew, Greek, and Latin warning of death for any Gentile or otherwise unclean person who dared to intrude further into the Temple.

The Festivals

In a Bible dictionary, look up *ark* or *ark of the covenant* (the receptacle for the tables of the Ten Commandments). If the people thought God actually resided in the Temple, what would be the significance of the destruction of the Temple?

On the east side was the Court of Women open to those who were ceremonially pure. The Court of Israel surrounded three sides and was separated by a low wall from the Court of the Priests. The great altar for burnt sacrifices, approximately fifty feet square, stood in this court. On one side were marble tables where the sacrificial animals were slaughtered. The sacrifices consisted of an unblemished male lamb, as well as a cereal (grain) and drink offering. On the sabbath, the sacrifices were doubled. On festival days, large numbers of animals were consumed.

The Temple was supported by a tax on every Jewish male over twenty years of age, supplies of wood required from the people, and freewill offerings. These revenues were used largely to purchase animals for the daily sacrifices. The priests and Levites who were employed full-time in the Temple were supported by proceeds from the hides of sacrificed animals, meat that was not fully consumed by the fires, and tithes from the people. The office of high priest was one of great prestige and power after Israel's return from the Exile. Since the Jews no longer had kings, the high priests assumed some of the trappings of royalty.

The Festivals

Quickly review the major festivals. These festivals are the celebrations that made up the core of Jesus' religious upbringing.

What are the central and formative religious festivals in Christianity? What do they mean to you religiously? Does our secularization of these holy days influence their impact on our faith? If so, how?

The Jewish calendar, in which months were counted by the moon, provides for several annual feasts of great importance to the religion. *Rosh Hashanah* is the Jewish New Year and the beginning of a series of holy days. *Yom Kippur*, the Day of Atonement, is a time for Jews to fast and pray for forgiveness. As long as the Temple was in existence, the high priest officiated over special sacrifices. On that day only, the high priest entered into the Holy of Holies to sprinkle the blood

Look back to Exodus 12–13 and forward to Luke 2:41-51. Using a Bible dictionary, get a more complete picture of how the Passover was celebrated and how Jesus participated in it. Jesus was steeped in his religious tradition of salvation history. Think about the nature of your own religious upbringing. Invite those who have been in the church since childhood to reflect on how that lifelong practice has influenced their adulthood and their ongoing faith journey.

of sacrificial animals as offering for the sins of the people.

The Feast of Booths or Tabernacles, *Succoth*, is a remembrance of God's providence during the years of wandering in the wilderness after the Exodus. The rededication of the Temple after the Maccabean defeat of the Seleucids in 166 B.C. is commemorated at *Hannukah*, the Feast of Lights or Dedication. The heroism of Esther and the Jews' victory over their Persian persecutors is celebrated in the holiday of *Purim*. The Feast of Unleavened Bread, *Mazzoth*, had been combined by the time of Jesus with Passover, *Pesach*, commemorating the events around the Exodus. *Shavuoth* is the Feast of Weeks, a festival of the harvest. Every male Jew was to travel to Jerusalem for the Feasts of Booths, Passover, and the Feast of Weeks.

The Synagogue ■

The Synagogue

Synagogues probably developed during the Exile when the people were without the Temple. They were places for both learning and worship. By the time of Christ, every community had its own synagogue. The life of the synagogue was focused on the reading, study, and interpretation of Scripture. The chief worship service was held on the sabbath morning. It consisted of the recitation of the *Shema* (Deuteronomy 6:4-9), prayer, Scripture reading in Hebrew, translation into the Aramaic or Greek that the congregation would understand, interpretation or preaching, and blessing. The early Christians used this synagogue worship pattern as they fashioned their services of worship. After the destruction of the Temple and end of the sacrificial system in A.D. 70, the synagogue became the most significant public institution in Jewish life.

Religious and Political Parties ■

Form groups of five or six people. Two will be *amme ha-retz* ("just folks"); the other four will be members of one of the various parties. Now identify a "hot topic" within the church or society (abortion, homosexuality, gun control, welfare reform, health-care reform, campaign-finance policies, for example). Staying in your own role, how would you argue for or against your hot topic issue?

Religious and Political Parties

First-century Judaism contained groups of persons with a diversity of views and practices. The points of most obvious disagreement were (1) attitude toward the law and (2) attitude toward Roman authority.

The most influential group was the Pharisees. They probably developed out of the Hasidim or "pious ones" who helped inspire the Maccabean Revolt and supported the Hasmonean dynasty. Laymen, not priests, they so honored the law of God that they stressed its precise application to every detail of life. They developed a body of tradition or oral law by studying the decisions of earlier teachers and applying them to new situations, even when such application required speculation and use of analogy.

Intense students of the Scriptures, they expanded interpretation and "built a fence around the law" by requiring such meticulous obedience that one would not even come close to violating it. Ardent observers of the sabbath and of ritual purity, they saw themselves as public examples of correct behavior. Pharisees believed in angels as mediators between God and humans and in resurrection. Most of them saw their nation's domination by the Romans and Herod as punishment from God and believed that God would ultimately intervene and bring deliverance. At their worst they so feared transgressing the law that they became narrowly legalistic and judgmental toward other Jews. At their best they reinterpreted and reapplied the law in ways that kept Judaism vital and growing.

The Sadducees, a smaller group, represented the highest levels of the priesthood and of the aristocratic families. Quite influential in the Sanhedrin (a political court

Analyze the interpersonal dynamics in the debate you had. How did the various divergent roles influence your conversation, your ability to agree or to compromise, and your level of respect for each other's position? If Jesus were to have entered your group, what might have been his position?

presided over by the high priest; it may have had legislative functions as well), they were known for strict judgments in judicial proceedings. They were rather literalistic in their interpretation of Scripture. For them, only the Pentateuch was normative, and the authority of the oral law was completely rejected. Sadducees did not believe in angels, spirits, or resurrection. Politically, they usually co-operated with the Romans. The group was weakening in the early first century and disappeared after the destruction of the Temple.

While the New Testament relates some of Jesus' interactions with both Pharisees and Sadducees, there is no mention of the Essenes. This sectarian group is known through the documents and archeological discoveries at Qumran. The Essenes rejected worship in the Temple believing it to be corrupted by an illegitimate priesthood and an inaccurate calendar. Most of them withdrew into the wilderness around the Dead Sea and formed monastic communities where they practiced a strict discipline of holiness. Clearly there were differing groups within the Essenes. For example, most practiced celibacy; but at least one group married. All seem to have understood themselves as a community of the end times, called out by God to prepare for the last great battle against evil.

The Zealots believed that God demanded unconditional resistance to the rule of Rome. They refused to pay Roman taxes and were willing to use violence as an instrument of doing God's will. The only record of their existence as a party with the name *Zealot* is in the writings of the Jewish historian Josephus. Although it may have been in the A.D. 66–70 period that they emerged as a group, their convictions can be traced back to many who resisted Rome and Herod earlier. In Luke 6:15 one of Jesus' disciples is identified as "Simon, who was called the Zealot."

Not surprisingly, the vast majority of the Jewish people did not fit into any of these parties. They were known as the *amme haretz*, the people of the land. They were ordinary hard-working people, looked down upon by some because they were not conscientious about observing the minutia of the law. In general they had apocalyptic hopes, believing that God would intervene to deliver them and defeat evil. These were the people among whom Jesus ministered most.

Apocalypticism

Apocalyptic theology looked for the imminent end of the present age, when God would step into history in a dramatic and definitive way. This kind of thought flourishes in situations in which people are oppressed and see no way out, except for God to destroy the forces of evil and vindicate the righteous. Apocalyptic sections appear in many books of the Bible, but Daniel 7–12 and all of the Book of Revelation are obvious examples.

Can He Be the Messiah?

Why do you think the Jewish people have suffered such repeated and severe persecution throughout their history? Look back at the timeline. What events in particular would create in them a yearning for a messiah?

"He Cannot Be the Messiah, Can He?"

Just as there was no one stream of belief and practice in Judaism, there was no common agreed-upon expectation of a Messiah. All Jews in the first century, as they had for so many years, longed for freedom and a better life for themselves and their nation. But, there was little clarity about how this might come to pass and little agreement about what form God's action might take.

In the Old Testament the word *Messiah* (Hebrew *mashiah*), which in Greek is *Christos*, appears thirty-nine times. In most of these

Some Jews look for a political messiah, which Jesus certainly was not. Read Isaiah 52:13–15; Jeremiah 23:5-8; and Exekiel 34:11-24—all of which are interpreted with messianic overtones. What do these prophetic passages tell us about the one whom God will send and anoint?

Obviously, not all Jews believed that Jesus was the Messiah, but Christians and Jews cannot deny deep and common roots. What is the appropriate (the "Christian") attitude for Christians to have toward Jews and Judaism? Should we be actively trying to convert Jews to Christianity? Why or why not?

Closing Prayer ■

Jesus, as a Jew, was steeped in religious festivals that included prayer and the celebration of God's mighty acts in this salvation history. Take a moment to consider your own place in this history and to make or renew a personal covenant with Christ.

Join in your circle prayer, praying for your faithfulness to God's unfolding plans.

places, the term clearly is referring to the reigning king of Israel. The word means "anointed." Israel's kings were anointed with olive oil poured upon their head and came to be known as "the Lord's anointed" or "the anointed one." First Samuel 10:1 relates Samuel's anointing of Saul as king; chapter sixteen recounts the anointing of David.

The term is also used in some of the royal psalms—those that were dedicated to the king. Eventually *Messiah* may have been used for a future king who would be an ideal ruler. Jeremiah 23:5-8 and Ezekiel 34:11-24 are examples of references to the coming king as a descendant of David. There is less emphasis on the Messiah in Hebrew Scripture than Christians have often thought.

The hope that God would send a Messiah grew more fervent in the first-century period. The end of the Hasmonean dynasty, the conquest of the Holy Land by Rome, and the harsh reign of Herod caused many Jews to look ever more desperately for divine deliverance. Still, there was no widespread agreement on how this deliverance might happen. Certainly there was no paradigm of what the Messiah might be like. Probably most Jews were praying for a powerful human ruler who would lead them in the overthrow of their oppressors and restore Israel to prominence and prosperity.

Session Three

In the Days of Augustus and Herod

Session Focus ■

Faith, be it Jewish or Christian, does not enjoy the luxury of existing in isolation from all of the other aspects of human life. The Mediterranean world was a very different place in the first century A.D. than it had been in the sixth century B.C. The cultural world into which Jesus and Christianity were born was not only Jewish but also Hellenistic. Politically, that world was dominated by the Roman Empire and the puppet rulers who were instruments of Rome's control.

Session Objective ■

The objectives of this session are to fill in the historical gaps between the Old and New Testaments; to recognize and understand one of the significant themes of both Matthew and Luke's infancy narratives (the conflict of power between secular political authority and the authority of God in Jesus Christ); and to apply these insights to our lives as individuals and as a society today.

The world into which Jesus was born was politically a Roman world and culturally a Hellenistic one. The historical background of the New Testament is much simpler than that of the Old. Rather than trying to keep track of empires and conquests, kings and exiles, the New Testament reader only needs to acquire a basic understanding of the Greco-Roman setting that is the context for not only the birth of Christ but also his ministry, execution, and resurrection. The early Christian church developed within this Greco-Roman world for most of the first five centuries of its existence. Every New Testament book, whether it makes any reference to historical events or not, was influenced by the former glory and grandeur of the Greco-Roman setting.

Historical Background After the Exile

In 539 B.C., the empire of Persia conquered the Babylonians who had taken the people of Judah into Exile. Cyrus, the Persian king, not only allowed the Jews to return to their homeland but also aided them in the rebuilding of the Temple. He returned to the Jews the gold and silver vessels that Nebuchadnezzar, the Babylonian king, had taken from Solomon's Temple (Ezra 5).

Session Preparation ■

Collect some newspaper and news magazine articles that illustrate conflict in the contemporary world between secular and spiritual authority.

Read 1 Maccabees 4–5 and 2 Maccabees 6–7 in the Apocrypha.

Read the theologically powerful short story entitled "The Displaced Person," by Flannery O'Connor. It can be found in almost any collection of her stories.

Choose from among these activities and discussion starters to plan your lesson.

Historical ■
Background

Return to the timeline begun in Session 2 and update it. Include the return from Exile and the beginning and end of Alexander's Empire. As other significant dates are mentioned throughout the session, add them as well.

Read Isaiah 45:1-8. What is God's commission to Cyrus? Who is in charge? Why has God given Cyrus this commission?

Bible 301 ☐

Look up Alexander and Hellenism (or related words, such as Greece or Greeks) in an encyclopedia or Bible dictionary. What was the extent of Alexander's empire? What were the highlights of Hellenism? What made these cultural characteristics so objectionable to the Jews?

Isaiah 45:1 speaks of Cyrus as God's "anointed" (also correctly translated as "messiah"). While Persian rule was certainly less harsh than had been the Babylonian, the Jews struggled against poverty. There were no Jewish kings during this period. The high priests functioned as the rulers under Persian overlordship. The historical books of the Old Testament come to an end at this point in Jewish history.

The period between what is recorded in the Old Testament and what is recorded in the New is called the intertestamental period. It covers about four centuries during which the Jewish people lived mostly under the rule of enemy empires. In the early fourth century B.C., the armies of Alexander the Great overthrew the Persian Empire and went on to conquer as far as India and the limits of the universe were known to exist by Western people of the time.

Alexander was a student of the great Greek philosopher Aristotle. Alexander was apparently a man of intellectual curiosity himself. He understood his mission not only to conquer but also to spread over the world the language and culture of Greece, which he believed to be far superior to any other in existence. Alexander's missionary efforts were quite successful. Although he died very suddenly and prematurely (in 323 B.C.), his influence resulted in Greek language and culture becoming pervasive throughout most of his empire. These Greek elements combined with the indigenous cultures of the various peoples he conquered forming the blend known as Hellenism. (*Hellene* was an ancient name for the Greeks.) Palestine was a tiny part of Alexander's empire, and Hellenistic culture

What turn of events under
Antiochus IV Epiphanes
changed the situation of
the Jews?

Read Leviticus 11:7-8 and
recall Bible stories that
include pigs (such as the
prodigal son). Of the speci-
fied "unclean" animals not
to be used for food, the pig
is probably the most promi-
nent. What is the significance of a Jew having contact with swine? Read further in Leviticus 11 to find
what must be done to
cleanse oneself from con-
tact with unclean things.

Read Daniel 9:20-27, an
apocalyptic reference to
three years of Antiochus's
reign, and Matthew 24:15-
28. What would you con-

influenced the life and thought of its Jewish
population.

Antiochus IV and the Maccabees

After Alexander's death, his empire was
split into parts by his chief generals who
warred with each other for supremacy. Two
in particular gained ascendancy: Ptolemy
and Seleucus. Palestine is located in a pivotal and perilous place. It forms a land
bridge connecting Egypt in the south to the
various empires of the Mesopotamia /
Fertile Crescent area. Throughout history,
Palestine has been used as a military high-
way for enemy nations moving to invade
each other. Between the Ptolemaic power in
Egypt and the Seleucid might in Syria, the
land of the Jews was a place of contention
and conflict.

Ultimately the Seleucids won control over
Palestine. One of their emperors, Antiochus
IV, named himself "Epiphanes," meaning
"god made manifest." He was intent upon
imposing Hellenistic culture upon all of his
empire. Some of the aristocratic Jews accepted and approved. But most of the Jewish
people were outraged at Hellenistic practices
that included veneration of other gods.
Antiochus IV Epiphanes thought that
Judaism was an inferior religion and decided
to stamp it out

In a brutal effort, perhaps surpassed only
by the Holocaust in World War II, Jewish
religious practices were declared illegal. It
was a capital offense to possess a copy of
Torah or to circumcise an infant. These pro-
hibitions were enforced by executions, tor-
tures, and other atrocities. A statue of the
Greek god Zeus was erected, and Jews were
forced to make offerings to it.

The Temple was desecrated; a pig, an ani-

sider to be a "desolating sacrifice" in your place of worship? What might be the utmost limit that could be imposed on you and your faith before you would either rebel or have to admit acquiescence? What level of resistance might you be prepared to offer if you were not only denied the right to worship as you wished but also were actively and brutally oppressed because of it?

Bible 301 ☐

Share some of the stories found in First and Second Maccabees. How does knowing this history influence your attitude toward first-century Jews? your understanding of the world into which God sent the Son?

The Romans and King Herod ■

Add the key dates and events to your timeline.

mal that the Jews believed to be unclean (see Leviticus 11:7-8), was sacrificed on the great altar. This act of defilement was so extreme that it was seared into the minds of Jewish people. It is what Jesus was speaking of in Matthew 24:15 and Mark 13:14. Daniel 9:27, which was written soon after this terrible period, refers to "an abomination that desolates." All Jews caught being faithful to God were cruelly slaughtered.

Finally a revolt broke out, under the leadership of Mattathias and his five sons. Judas, the oldest son, became known as "Maccabeus" or "The Hammer." He and other members of this family, called the Maccabees, led a twenty-four-year revolt against the Seleucids. The success of this revolt and the reclamation of the Temple are celebrated annually by Jews as Hanukkah, the Feast of Lights.

Under the rule of the Hasmonean line of kings, descendants of the Maccabees, Israel enjoyed about 130 years of independence, although some of these rulers betrayed their heritage and cooperated with the Hellenizers rather than with the faithful Jews. But soon Palestine was threatened by a new empire, which would become larger and more powerful than any in the past. In 63 B.C., the Roman general Pompey laid siege to Jerusalem and killed many priests. After three months, Rome overcame the Jewish resistance and took control of the city. The life of Christ and the beginning of Christianity took place during the two centuries of Rome's greatest power throughout the Mediterranean world.

The Romans and King Herod

Widespread Hellenism provided the Mediterranean world with a language and culture shared by many groups of people. *Koine*, or common Greek, served as a universal language. The might of Rome enforced general peace and order through well-organized governance and military occupation. The Empire developed a fine network of roads and ships to facilitate easier and more rapid transportation and communication. Religious toleration allowed a multiplicity of diverse religions and philosophies. The Jews benefited from Rome's toleration, which allowed them free practice of their faith, some self-government, and exemption from military duty.

The *Pax Romana*, or Roman peace, which lasted for some two hundred years, was broken chiefly by the Jews in Palestine. In 37 B.C., Rome designated Herod as the king of the Jews. Actually he was a vassal or puppet king, beholden and accountable to Rome, as were the others who governed the Jews after him. Although he claimed some Jewish blood, his ascension to power was bitterly opposed, especially in Galilee. Even with Roman help it took him three years to conquer the land. With his rule established, Herod the Great turned to extensive, massive building projects. Roman-ruled Jerusalem boasted grand Hellenistic cities. Theaters, gymnasiums, shrines, monuments, fortresses, and palaces were among Herod's projects. Herod rebuilt the Temple in Jerusalem in imposing style, making it a magnificent, richly appointed place of Jewish worship.

The Jews hated Herod for his elaborate homage to the emperor as a deity and for the golden eagle that he had erected in front of the Temple. The huge building projects were supported by a heavy burden of both tribute and labor imposed on the people. Herod's

Use a Bible dictionary or encyclopedia to look up more details on Herod the Great. What was he like? What kind of ruler was he? What were some of the reasons why he was so feared and despised by the Jews? What relationship did he claim to have with the Jews? What elements are brewing that would lead to trouble and to the expectation and hope for a messiah?

rule was also harsh and oppressive. Through the use of military force and treacherous informants, he presided over a brutal police state.

The Jewish people revolted against Rome four times in less than a century and a half, until the final destruction of Jerusalem in A.D. 135. Two of these revolts occurred around the time of Jesus' birth, another before the gospels of Matthew or Luke were written, and the last before these Gospels were widely known. Herod's death in 4 B.C., soon after Jesus' birth, was the occasion of a major uprising involving almost every Jewish district. The forces of Herod and his successors, bolstered by the support of Roman troops, suppressed all of these rebellions with slaughter, pillage, and bondage. Sepphoris, the chief city in Galilee located not far from Nazareth, was captured, burned, and its inhabitants enslaved. Two thousand rebels were hunted out of the hill country and crucified by the Romans.

Herod's power as king of the Jews, upheld by the Roman authority, was immense; and he exercised it ambitiously and shrewdly. Not only did he hold military, economic, and political powers, but he also exerted control in the religious life of the Jews. Casting aside the hereditary priesthood that Judaism had honored for centuries, Herod appointed a priestly aristocracy that was beholden to him. His illegitimate claim to kingship caused the revolts against Herod's authority to take messianic form. Rebel leaders claimed that they represented the authentic kingship promised by God. The goal of rebellion was the overthrow of the power of Herod and of Rome, liberation for the Jewish people, and rule by a leader raised up by God.

The Conflict of Kingdoms in Matthew

It is against this historical backdrop that we must see the events around the birth of Jesus. Both Matthew and Luke develop the theme of opposition between two authorities—that of Herod and Rome against that of God. Matthew traces the genealogy of Jesus through the line of Israel's kings so as to present him as the authentic successor to the throne of David.

The Wise Men

What do you recall about the wise men? Where were they from? What were their names? How many were there?

Now read Matthew 2:1-12. What is the biblical record about the wise men? How much of what you "know" is from legend or hymnody? from the Bible?

How and where do you see God intervening with and guiding the wise men? What does this mean to you?

The Wise Men and Herod

When the wise men came to Herod's court in their search for the newborn Jesus, they inquired, "Where is the child who has been born king of the Jews?" (Matthew 2:2). It is this designation that so frightened Herod. It appeared that a rival king had been born, and he was determined to find and kill him. It is only by the intervention of God who sent warning dreams to both the wise men and to Joseph that the infant Christ escaped Herod's sword. There is no historical record of a slaughter of male infants in and around Bethlehem, but such an occurrence in that obscure part of the Empire would have attracted little attention outside the vicinity. Certainly Herod was capable of such an action. In his paranoia, he had many persons killed, including his wife and two of his sons. The quotation in Matthew 2:18 is from the words of the Old Testament prophet Jeremiah (31:15). Rachel was the wife of the patriarch Jacob and the mother of Joseph and Benjamin. According to Scripture, her grave is located near Bethlehem. In Jeremiah she is portrayed as mourning the defeat and exile of Judah by the empire of Babylon.

The town of Ramah, located north of Jerusalem, had been used as a collection point for the people who were being transported into exile in other parts of the Empire. The danger and suffering associated with the birth of the Christ Child is seen as a kind of reenactment of the ancient tragedy for the nation.

The Flight to Egypt ■
Read Matthew 2:16-23. How do you see God intervening on behalf of the Holy Family? What would this story of flight (or exodus or exile) have meant to the Jews? What does it mean to you to think that Jesus and his family had to flee for their lives?

The last several decades of the twentieth century have witnessed the displacement of huge numbers of persons from their homelands, usually due to warfare. Many of these people are perpetual refugees; they and their children live and die in camps and temporary settlements. What could be the significance to these refugees of the Holy Family's flight to Egypt? What does this story say to those of us who are in much more fortunate circumstances?

The Flight to Egypt

While Matthew is proclaiming the coming of a new ruler, he makes very clear that the circumstances of this king's birth were anything but royal. The story of the flight into Egypt may not be historically factual, but it is a powerful portrayal of the violent opposition of earthly authorities to the one who will inaugurate the reign of God. Mary, Joseph, and the Child were forced to flee from a tyrant determined to annihilate his rival. In 2:19-22, the Holy Family is pictured as refugees from oppression, as persons displaced from their home and forced to flee for their lives. Many who read Matthew's Gospel in the period during and after A.D. 66–70 had similar experiences.

As the Roman army besieged and captured Jerusalem, destroyed the Temple, and forced many to leave their homeland, Jewish Christians must have been able to identify with the Christ, who even as a tiny infant had been the victim of similar violence. Stories of massacres, fugitives, and weeping were their life stories as well. The dispossessed and downtrodden of all ages in this account are promised that they will ultimately be delivered by God who will overturn the dominant powers who oppress and destroy.

Jesus, ■
the New Moses
The stories of Jesus and Moses are linked, among other ways, by time spent in Egypt. What are other links and parallels? Read

Jesus, the New Moses

Matthew suggests strong parallels between the birth of Jesus and the Old Testament story of the birth of Moses. Again the theme is that of conflict of kingdoms. In Exodus 1:8–2:10, Pharaoh ordered the death of all

Exodus 1:8–2:10 and review Matthew 2:1-23.

newborn Hebrew boys. The midwives, Shiphrah and Puah, disobeyed Pharaoh's command. They did not kill the babies, and they lied to Pharaoh to protect them. The wise men in Matthew behaved rather like these midwives. They disobeyed Herod's command to return and tell him the whereabouts of the infant King. Both the midwives and the magi recognized the conflict between powers; both chose to resist human authority figures in order to protect infants who represent the authority of God.

How did bold acts of defiance aid Moses and Jesus? What risks did these key persons face? When and under what circumstances do you think such risk would be appropriate for you?

In the Exodus account, God's work is done by three more women who acted outside of the accepted bounds of behavior. Moses' mother risked her own life by concealing his birth and placing him in a basket on the river. His sister Miriam, who later joined her brother in a role of leadership, took the risk of following the little basket on the river and approaching the royal woman who found it. Pharaoh's daughter chose to adopt this child whom she must have known was one of the Hebrew boys that her father had ordered killed. In the narratives of Jesus' infancy, Mary (and in Luke, Elizabeth as well) chose to obey God and accept the role to which she had been called.

What are the conflicts of power as presented by Matthew?

In an earlier period of oppression God raised up Moses. During the oppression by Rome and Herod, God was raising up a new (and greater) Moses to lead the people to freedom. The motif is accentuated by the Holy Family's flight into Egypt. Matthew uses this episode to link Jesus to another Old Testament prophecy. In this case, it is in Hosea 11:1 in which God is speaking of the nation Israel, "Out of Egypt I called my son."

Underlying the events related in Matthew 2:1-23 is the sharp contrast between those who occupy the seats of power and those who are victimized by that power. For Matthew a new king, indeed, has been born—a king whose authority will be exercised to uplift the downtrodden and liberate the oppressed.

The Conflict of Kingdoms in Luke

The Conflict of Kingdoms in Luke

Does the disparity between Luke and Matthew on Jesus' hometown make any difference to the Jesus story? to you? Explain.

The chronology and events of the infancy narratives in Matthew and Luke cannot be brought into harmony without great distortion of the texts. Indeed, to attempt to combine the two into one story is to diminish the meaning of both. Matthew assumes that Bethlehem is the hometown of Mary and Joseph and, hence, the place where the Christ Child is born. With his customary insistence upon closely linking Jesus with Hebrew Scriptures, Matthew quotes Micah 5:2, which he understands as a prophecy of the birth of the Messiah in Bethlehem. It is only when the family returns from their place of sanctuary in Egypt that they go to Nazareth to live, because it is in a safer area than Bethlehem (2:22-23).

Luke presents the opposite pattern. Nazareth is assumed to be the hometown of Mary and Joseph. They must travel to Bethlehem to meet the requirements of a Roman census. The Christ Child is born while they are there (Luke 2:4-6) and, assumedly, they return to Nazareth soon after.

The Census and Taxes

The Census and Taxes

Add these key dates (or approximations of dates) for the various rulers and the census.

Luke has theological, rather than historical, reasons for using the Roman census as the backdrop of his story of the Nativity. In chapter two he begins by setting the Christ story in the context of world history. The ruling Roman emperor is Augustus; the governor of Syria, the province of which Judea

Read Luke 2:1-7. Do the variations in dating that call into dispute the absolute historical accuracy of Luke's narrative make any significant difference in the gospel story? to you? Explain. What is Luke's theological point? What is the conflict between kingdoms for Luke?

was a part, is Quirinius. The census is said to be for "all the world" (verse 1). Some parts of this setting are historically accurate; others reveal Luke's method and purpose in writing.

Augustus (earlier known as Octavian) was Caesar or emperor from 44 / 42 B.C. until A.D. 14. Quirinius, however, did not become governor of Syria until A.D. 6 at which time he did order a census of Judea (also mentioned in Acts 5:37). Luke is using these later events as a part of the setting of his narrative without concern for precise dating, because they help him develop his theme. The census referred to in Luke 2:1-5 would not have been conducted as Luke describes. While Rome certainly demanded tribute, Roman taxation did not involve having persons return to their family's place of origin. While Herod the Great ruled, the Romans gave him responsibility for the census.

The significance of distinguishing Luke's account from a purely historical version is that it allows readers to realize the theological understandings with which Luke is so concerned. As in Matthew, one of the themes of the infancy narratives is to emphasize the conflict of kingdoms. The heavy tribute or tax required by Rome and its puppet rulers such as Herod was always a focal point of Jewish resentment and rebellion. The census decree in Luke's story represents the overall system of subjugation under which the Jewish people lived.

From the House of David

Form four groups, each to read a different passage: Luke 2:1-11; 2 Samuel 7:1-17; Isaiah 9:1-7; and Isaiah 11:1-9. What do these verses say about the house and family of David?

One From the House of David

Luke is proclaiming the coming of a ruler who will, by God's power, oppose and overturn these systems. The Christ Child is the anointed king from David's lineage who will deliver Israel from oppression. Joseph, Jesus' legal father, is "descended

What will be the characteristics of the restored kingdom of David? How would this contrast with the rule of Caesar and the house of Herod?
The promise of a Davidic king was longstanding and a long time in coming—over five hundred years. How could hope be sustained all those years? What hopeful signs do you see of a reign of peace under God? What sustains you? To which of God's promises do you cling in times of trouble?

Bible 301 ☐

Mr. Guizac, the Polish refugee, is a Christ figure in The Displaced Person. *Consider what he shows us about Christ. To stimulate discussion, analyze two of Mrs. McIntyre's comments: "I am not responsible for the world's misery" and "He didn't have to come in the first place." What do these characters reveal to us about ourselves?*

from the house and family of David" (2:4). The angels announce the birth that happened in Bethlehem, "the city of David." Jewish Christians understood immediately the significance of descent from King David.

A thousand years before the birth of Christ, David, despite his moral lapses, was understood to be God's chosen ruler. In 2 Samuel 7:8-9, 16 God spoke to David through the prophet Nathan:

"I took you from the pasture, from following the sheep to be prince over my people Israel; and I have been with you wherever you went, and have cut off all your enemies from before you; and I will make for you a great name, like the name of the great ones of the earth. . . . Your house and your kingdom shall be made sure forever before me; your throne shall be established forever."

The "house" or dynasty of David had been interrupted, perhaps ended, in 587 B.C. when the Babylonians conquered Judah. The Hebrews continued to believe that God would honor this covenant with David. The Messiah, God's anointed ruler, would surely be from the house of David. In Isaiah 9:7 the prophet describes the ideal king who is coming to reign: "His authority shall grow continually, / and there shall be endless peace / for the throne of David and his kingdom. / He will establish and uphold it with justice and with righteousness / from this time onward and forevermore." A similar description of the messianic king in Isaiah 11 begins, "A shoot shall come out from the stump of Jesse [David's father], / and a branch shall grow out of his roots." These and other prophetic utterances affirm that

God's chosen deliverer of Israel will be a descendant of David. The authority and reign of this ruler—peaceful, just, and righteous—will stand in sharp contrast to the rule of Caesar.

Rome's Pax and God's Peace

As another way of contrasting God's ruler and the Roman emperor, Luke focuses on the concept of "peace." Under Caesar Augustus the Roman Empire had become so dominant that there was little armed resistance and few internal revolts. Peace was imposed upon the world by the military power of Rome. Historians apply the term *Pax Romana* (or Roman peace) to this long period without war. A part of the Roman reverence of Caesar was to acclaim him as the person who brought about and maintained peace. Luke's message is starkly different: Only Jesus Christ brings real peace to the people of the world. The angels announce that peace that has come from "God in the highest heaven" (Luke 2:14). Such a proclamation was a direct challenge to imperial authority. Caesar's peace is false and based upon military strength; God's peace is authentic and comes through Jesus Christ.

As a way of enforcing allegiance to the Empire, Rome demanded homage to the emperor as a deity. In this worship of Caesar, the emperor's birthday was celebrated as "good news for the whole world." In Luke 2:10, the angel tells the shepherds of the birth that is "good news of great joy for all the people." In verse 11, the angel calls the newborn child "Savior," a term very rarely applied to Jesus in the Synoptic Gospels. Surely Luke is countering the claims of Augustus who was widely called Savior as a

Rome's Pax and God's Peace ■

How does Luke use a kind of dual theme or play on words in his use of the word *peace*? What kind of peace does Jesus Christ bring to the world? Where do you see it?

Share and discuss your news articles about conflict between secular and spiritual powers today. How can Christians enter into this conflict on the right side?

Bible 301 ☐

Read Romans 13:1-3a in which Paul writes to Christians to be subject to ruling authorities. Regardless of what Paul might have meant by these words, they have been used historically by repressive governments to justify themselves and to warn their subjects against rebellion. What is the proper relationship between Christians and governing authorities?

part of the worship of his divinity. In the infancy narratives of Luke a major theme is Jesus' challenge to oppressive, earthly authorities. In the life and work of God's Messiah will be found true peace, joy, liberation, and salvation.

Closing Prayer ■

Jesus, the Prince of Peace, entered a troubled world that is still troubled. His coming invites others into a new Kingdom. Take a moment to think about your own "membership" and participation in this Kingdom and to make or renew your personal relationship with Jesus Christ.

Close with your circle prayer and include prayers for all refugees, displaced persons, and world leaders to find an honest, respectable, and lasting peace.

Session Four

Righteous Before God

Session Focus ■

Zechariah, Elizabeth, and Joseph play what might be considered minor roles in the birth narrative of Jesus, but they set the stage for great things to come. In addition, they help us and their own community bridge the gap between the promises of God for salvation and the fulfillment of that promise.

Session Objective ■

This session will explore the expectations of the Messiah and the figures who played a part in introducing the Messiah to the world. We will become acquainted with these three persons as well as the Old Testament figures whose memory and works they evoke.

Session Preparation ■

This session includes two excerpts from the Protevangelion, which do not claim to be Gospel, but are extra-biblical material that may help to shed light on the traditions of Mary and Joseph. If you have access to a copy, read chapters 1–8 in order to learn more about these traditions. (*See The Lost Books of the Bible*.)

Zechariah, Elizabeth, and Joseph each play what we would consider a minor role in the dramatic story told in the infancy narratives. They may be thought of as the supporting cast. Luke 1:6 introduces Zechariah and Elizabeth: "Both of them were righteous before God, living blamelessly according to all the commandments and regulations of the Lord." Matthew describes Joseph similarly, though more briefly, as "a righteous man" (Matthew 1:19). The Gospel writers are telling us that these three persons were notable for their integrity and uprightness. Specifically, this description emphasizes that all three are persons who conscientiously obey the laws of God.

In the case of Zechariah and Elizabeth, Luke may think that it is necessary to state this explicitly because childlessness was considered an indication of sin, particularly on the part of a barren woman. Matthew wants to make clear that the man chosen to be the legal father of Christ is an obedient servant of God, a strict observer of the law.

The story of Elizabeth and Zechariah, the parents of John the Baptist, is told nowhere other than in Luke's Gospel. Even here, the story is confined to the first chapter, and neither of the characters is mentioned again. In the larger scheme of Luke's account, however, Elizabeth and Zechariah are quite significant. They form a kind of bridge between

Righteous Before God

Read Luke 1:5-7 and Matthew 2:18-19 for a brief introduction to Zechariah, Elizabeth, and Joseph. What other biblical characters do you recall being described as "righteous"? What is *righteousness*? Who do you know whom you would consider righteous?

A Priest Meets an Angel

Read Luke 1:5-13. Look in your study Bible or in a Bible dictionary for a diagram of the Temple. Try to envision what each of the priests would be doing while the congregation was gathered, waiting for the benediction from the priest.

Envision Zechariah being visited by an angel and recall the obvious parallels with the angelic visit to Abram and Sarai (Genesis 12). What happened? How did Zechariah react?

Have you ever felt that God has touched you directly or through a "heaven-sent" mediator? If so, what was that experience like? What

the Old Testament and the New, setting the coming of Jesus in the context of earlier Hebrew history. In his commentary, Fred Craddock, writing in *Luke: Interpretation* (John Knox, 1990), asserts that a "fundamental conviction" of Luke is that "continuity with Israel's institutions, rituals, and faith puts one in position to be used for God's purpose. The old (in this case, an old couple) will issue in the new."

A Priest Meets an Angel

Zechariah is immediately introduced as a priest and so is associated with one of Judaism's most central institutions, the Temple, and with the most important part of Jewish worship, the sacrificial system. Like most of the thousands of priests in his day, Zechariah did not live in Jerusalem nor serve full-time in the Temple. Instead he traveled to the capital city only when it was his turn to serve. Jewish priests in this period were divided into twenty-four families or orders. Each order served in the Temple for two nonconsecutive weeks each year, in addition to the three great festivals when all priests were needed to handle the large number of sacrifices. Zechariah's family may have been very poor if they were dependent on a portion of the annual tithes given to the Temple.

On a typical day, the priests who were on duty in the Temple divided their duties by casting lots. This way it was determined who would clean the altar, prepare the cereal offering, slaughter the lamb, sprinkle the blood on the altar, and perform each of the other tasks involved in offering sacrifices on behalf of the people. On the day that he was addressed by the angel, Zechariah had been chosen by lot to be one of the five priests presenting the incense offering. This would

was the message? What lasting impact, if any, did that experience have on your life and faith?

John was to be a prophet, after nearly five hundred years of prophetic silence. What impact would this news have on a people who had historically relied on messages from God through the prophets?

Do you think you would have been prepared to listen after so much time of silence? Would you trust that this person was who he claimed to be? How might doubts influence the work John was called to do? How do doubt and skepticism surface in religious circles today? What impact does it have?

The Nazarite Tradition

What are some of the characteristics of the Nazirite community? Can you think of any other "set apart" communities? What about their "apartness" facilitates their purposes?

Look at some of the other heroes of the Hebrew Scriptures from the Nazarite tradition. Read Judges 13:4-5, Judges 16, and 1 Samuel 1:9-15. Who took vows before God? What were those vows, and how were they kept?

surely have been the highest moment of his life as a priest. After they had burned incense on the altar in the sanctuary of the Temple, the priests would come out on the steps and bless the gathered people.

On the occasion recounted in Luke 1, Zechariah saw the angel Gabriel standing by the incense altar. Gabriel was one of the seven archangels recognized in Judaism in this period. He usually served as the messenger of God. Gabriel told the stunned Zechariah that his wife Elizabeth would bear their son who was to be named John, meaning "God is gracious" or "God has shown favor." The child would "be great in the sight of the Lord." He would grow up to be a prophet in the tradition of Elijah and would prepare the people for God's promised deliverance. This was, indeed, a stunning message: There had been no prophets in Israel since the time of Malachi (hence, the final book of Hebrew Scripture), some five hundred years earlier.

The Nazarite Tradition

John, the promised child, would live in the Nazirite tradition, as described in Numbers 6. Nazirites were persons who chose to "separate themselves to the Lord." They lived ascetically, denying themselves any luxuries. Nazirites avoided the consumption of intoxicating drinks and even any contact at all with grapes and grape products—staples of the Hebrew diet. In Luke 7:33, the adult John the Baptist is said to "come eating no bread and drinking no wine."

The hair of Nazirites was not cut, except to be used as sacrificial offering to God—their heads were "consecrated." They were persons set apart, holy in lifestyle and devotion to God. Two well-known figures in

What kinds of vows do we take today in religious / faith settings (such as baptismal vows)? How seriously do you consider these vows? Are they promises to live by and live up to or just part of some ritual to be forgotten? Explain.

Hebrew history were Nazirites also, and the stories of the announcement of their births are similar to that of John. In Judges 13:4-5, the mother of Samson is told that her son will be a Nazirite "who shall begin to deliver Israel from the hand of the Philistines." John will also participate in the deliverance of Israel by preparing the way for the Messiah.

The vow to keep the hair uncut is what lies behind the story of Samson and Delilah in Judges 16. When Samson's hair was cut, his vow to God was violated and he lost his gift of great strength. In 1 Samuel 1:9-15, Hannah prays for a son; and she promises God that, "I shall set him before you as a nazirite until the day of his death."

The Spirit of Elijah

What do you remember about Elijah and his ministry? How does John resemble him?

So many of the biblical events and figures behind those events hearken back to other heroes of the faith. What is the benefit of this kind of continuity?

We live in a time and society that prizes individuality. Do we lose anything by not having obvious "proteges" who carry on the fine traditions of earlier generations? Who are our heroes? Who speaks to us prophetically about the future?

Read 2 Kings 2:1-12. Imagine yourself as Elisha or one of Elijah's inner cir-

The Spirit of Elijah

The second Old Testament motif in Gabriel's description of the coming child is that he will minister "with the spirit and power of Elijah." John will be filled with this spirit—the Holy Spirit—even before his birth. All four of the Gospels mention the relationship between John the Baptist and Elijah. At some points the linkage is very close. For example, in Mark 1:6, John is described as "clothed with camel's hair, with a leather belt around his waist, and he ate locusts and wild honey." This description echoes that of Elijah in 2 Kings 1:8: "a hairy man, with a leather belt around his waist." At other points, John's Elijah-like role is de-emphasized; probably this comes from Christians who feared that John's followers might compete with those of Jesus. Certainly all of the Gospels portray John in the role of one who prepares the way for the coming of the Messiah.

The career of the prophet Elijah is recounted in 1 Kings 17:1–2 Kings 2:12. He

cle of friends who witnesses this dramatic end to his life. How might you have felt to see such a thing? How might you have felt to lose such a special person? How might you have regarded or experienced God in this event?

Now imagine yourself as a member of the crowd of family and friends who gathered to celebrate the presentation of the infant John at the Temple. You know these stories of Elijah, you hope for the Messiah, and you hear the prophecy of Zechariah (Luke 1:68-79). What thoughts and feelings might this event evoke? Why?

Have you been in a situation of having prayed or hoped desperately for something but were unprepared to recognize or accept the answer to that prayer? What do you expect of God in terms of your day-to-day life? What do you expect of your prayers?

was a mighty prophet, indeed. He worked miracles, cured the sick, raised the dead, defeated the prophets of the false god Baal in a dramatic contest, and condemned the sins of King Ahab and his wife Jezebel. To follow in that tradition was surely a great challenge! In 2 Kings 2:1-12 is the powerful story of Elijah's being taken up to heaven—in a "whirlwind" on "a chariot of fire and horses of fire."

Only one other person—Enoch in Genesis 5:24—was accorded this honor in lieu of death. The popular Negro spiritual "Swing Low, Sweet Chariot" is inspired by this story. Enslaved men and women, suffering and oppressed, wished fervently for another such manifestation of divine power. It was perhaps because of this supranatural ascension from the earth that Elijah was traditionally expected to return. Even today, many Jewish families at their Passover meal set a place at the table that is kept empty for Elijah, should the prophet return and join them.

In Malachi 3:1a, God says: "See, I am sending my messenger to prepare the way before me." And, "Lo, I will send the prophet Elijah before the great and terrible day of the LORD comes. He will turn the hearts of parents to their children and the hearts of children to their parents, so that I will not come and strike the land with a curse" (4:5-6). These words are equivalent to the angel's message to Zechariah in Luke 1:17 about his son's ministry: "With the spirit and power of Elijah he will go before him, to turn the hearts of parents to their children, and the disobedient to the wisdom of the righteous, to make ready a people prepared for the Lord."

Significantly, it is in the holy place of Israel that the good news of the coming

Bible 301 ☐

Read selected portions of 1 Kings 17:1–2 Kings 1:18 to get a better portrait of the career of Elijah. What did Elijah do? Who did he defy or support to do it? In what ways did God empower him for this ministry? When did he show weakness, and what did he do about it? Are Elijah's life and relationship with God a model for you? If so, in what ways are they a model?

Elizabeth Bears a Son ■

Elizabeth is one in a succession of special mothers (our matriarchs in the faith) who were thought to be barren. Among four groups, divide these Scriptures and do some research: Genesis 17:1-22 and 18:9-16; Genesis 25:19-28; Judges 13:2-25; and 1 Samuel 1:1-20.

In each of these stories, identify the person to whom God revealed the intention to allow conception. What special plan did God (or God's angel) announce that the woman would conceive? What is the significance of having previously barren women as instruments of God's will? What do these stories have in common? What do they reveal about God? about our need for God? What are

Messiah is first made known. Even in this astonishing moment, Zechariah's scepticism was so strong that he questioned the angel and, as a result, was rendered mute (see 1:20, 22, 62). Like so many of God's people throughout the centuries, Zechariah had prayed to God but was not expectant or prepared for God to answer. Perhaps the loss of his speech was not so much a punishment of Zechariah as a sign to assure him that Gabriel's word was true and would come to pass. Zechariah had forgotten the meaning of his own name—"God has remembered." Speechless, he was unable to give benediction to the people when he exited the holy place.

Elizabeth Bears a Son

Like her husband, Elizabeth was of a priestly family; indeed, her descent is from Aaron himself. She was also in a succession of barren Jewish women whose stories are told in the Bible. Sarah, wife of Abraham and mother of Isaac; Rebekah, wife of Isaac and mother of Jacob and Esau; and Hannah, wife of Elkanah and mother of Samuel are perhaps the best known. Failure to bear children was more than a personal heartache. An infertile woman was believed to be suffering under a curse from God; she was disgraced in the eyes of her community. But, like those earlier women, Elizabeth received the divine blessing of motherhood, which "took away the disgrace [she had] endured" (Luke 1:25).

When Elizabeth was some six (lunar) months pregnant, she was visited by her relative Mary, pregnant herself with Jesus. The unborn child in Elizabeth's womb leapt as he who would become John the Baptist responded to the unborn Christ. This is one of several ways that Luke celebrates the role

the similarities of Elizabeth and Mary's conceptions of John and Jesus with these earlier events in their history?

Read Luke 1:39-45. This is an early declaration of Jesus as Lord. What do you suppose it meant to these two women to know throughout their pregnancy that their children were destined for exceptional lives? If you have a child, what kind of expectations did you have for the child before he or she was born? If you are expecting a child, do you have certain expectations for her or him?

What are the hopes and fears parents have for their unborn children? If you knew in advance that your child would face the kind of life that either John or Jesus had, how do you think you would you feel? What would you do?

The Benedictus ▮

Read the Benedictus (Luke 1:68-79) and the Hebrew Scriptures preceding them (from Malachi and Isaiah). What events in Hebrew history does Zechariah refer to? How does this prophecy fit into the salvation history of the Hebrews? What does it promise or prophesy?

of John in God's plan of salvation, but at the same time underlines the fact that John is secondary to Jesus.

Elizabeth was "filled with the Holy Spirit" and spoke as a prophet, proclaiming that Mary's child is the Christ. Her words in verses 42-45 constitute a canticle or hymn of praise, much briefer than that of her husband later. Through the Holy Spirit she realized without being told the blessing that Mary had received and the blessedness of the child she carried. When she spoke of Mary as "the mother of my Lord," it was the first time in the account that the word *Lord* clearly referred to Jesus rather than to God.

The birth of John the Baptist has traditionally been observed on June 24, in association with the summer solstice. Whenever it occurred, the birth was celebrated with great joy. The child was circumcised and named on the eighth day of his life. Zechariah's afflictions disappeared, and he joined in the praising of God. Here (verse 65) and elsewhere in the biblical story, fear (or awe) is the human response to a display of divine power or presence. Such fear often motivates, rather than stifles, ardent praise of God.

The Benedictus

Zechariah, unable to bless the people after his encounter with the angel, was now able to bless God eloquently in one of the four (if we count the brief words of Elizabeth) canticles in the first two chapters of Luke. These verses (1:68-79) are very important in Luke's theme of continuity between what we call the Old and New Testaments. In them the ministry of John the Baptist is set as a continuation of the work of God in the salvation history of Israel and as a link to God's work in Christ. Even more obviously than his parents, John was a bridge between the old covenant and the new. He was the last of the Old Testament prophets and the first of the New Testament disciples.

The Benedictus is largely composed of material taken from various parts of the Hebrew Scriptures. In verses 68-75, the focus is upon God's sending of Jesus—"a mighty savior" in the line of King David, spoken of by the prophets. God is praised for the promise to Abraham and for the liberating event of the Exodus. God's anticipated acts will bring deliverance and the creation of conditions in which God's people will be able to serve God and to live righteously. In verses 76-79 the focus shifts to John. He will be the one who proclaims and prepares for this mighty act of God. The description of his task is taken from Malachi 3:1-2 and 4:5-6, which we have already mentioned. Isaiah 9:2 and 42:7 are also used.

Recall the points made in earlier sessions about the dualism between light and darkness. What will be John's role?

Perhaps the most powerful line is Luke 1:78b, which continues the theme of light out of darkness that was mentioned in the first session. It has been variously translated over the centuries in efforts to capture its beauty. The King James Version is perhaps most familiar, but it incorrectly uses the past tense: "The dayspring from on high hath visited us." The NRSV reads, "The dawn from on high will break upon us." Today's English Version reads, "He will cause the bright dawn of salvation to rise on us."

A Righteous Man

A Righteous Man ■

Read Matthew 1:18-25. Review what we know of Mary and Joseph's marriage arrangements.

Matthew's account of the birth of Jesus is written from the perspective of Joseph. It is Joseph whom the angel visits. Throughout Matthew's story, Joseph is the parent to whom the divine will is being revealed, who

Read the excerpt from the Protevangelion for another version of Joseph's introduction to Mary and to his task. (If you have access to the whole text, read all of chapter 8.) Compare this extra-biblical text with Matthew 1:18-25. What new twists does the Protevangelion add to the story?

What are the ways in this biblical narrative that Joseph appears as a "righteous man"? His position was extraordinary. How might you feel to know that your spouse or fiancé was called by God to some spectacular course of action that would quite possibly appear, at least at first, as disgraceful or peculiar for you? (In the Protevangelion, the opposite happens: Joseph is accused and tried for "defiling" Mary when it was clearly known that she was to remain "a Virgin out of the house of the Lord." She was tried as well; but only Joseph underwent the test. Both, of course, were vindicated.)

is obedient to God, and who initiates the actions necessary to protect his family. In 1:18, Mary is said to be "engaged to Joseph." Yet in the very next verse, Joseph is described as "her husband." Luke never uses the terms *husband* and *wife* but instead simply speaks of the couple as betrothed.

Our best knowledge of the customs of the Jews at this time indicates that marriage involved two steps. The arrangements for the union would have been made between Mary's father and Joseph, probably when Mary was about thirteen years of age. If this was Joseph's first marriage, he was probably between the ages of eighteen and twenty-four, although Joseph may have been a much older man.

The Protevangelion

According to the Protevangelion, a book included in a collection of ancient Christian writings omitted from the authorized New Testament (see "Bible 301," page 13), Mary had lived at the Temple from the age of three (7:1-3). "When she was twelve years of age, the priests met in a council, and said, Behold, Mary is twelve years of age; what shall we do with her, for fear lest the holy place of the Lord our God should be defiled?" [The onset of puberty would make her periodically unclean.] "Then replied the priests to Zacharias the high-priest, Do you stand at the alter of the Lord, and enter into the holy place, and make petitions concerning her, and whatsoever the Lord shall manifest unto you, that do. . . .

"And behold the angel of the Lord came to him, and said, Zacharias, Zacharias, Go forth and call together all the widowers among the people, and let every one of them bring his rod, and he by whom the Lord shall shew a sign shall be the husband of Mary. . . .

"The last rod was taken by Joseph, and behold

a dove proceeded out of the rod, and flew upon the head of Joseph. And the high-priest said, Joseph, Thou art the person chosen to take the Virgin of the Lord, to keep her for him: But Joseph refused, saying, I am an old man, and have children, but she is young, and I fear lest I should appear ridiculous in Israel. Then the high-priest replied, Joseph, fear the Lord thy God. . . . Joseph, then being afraid, took her unto his house" (8:3-4, 6, 11-14, 16).

Read through Luke 2 for instances of Joseph's quiet support. What does he do for his family and thus for God and for humankind? Have you ever known someone of that strength of character and courage? How has he or she helped to shape your faith?

There would be a formal exchange of consent by the couple, and the man henceforth had legal rights over the woman. This was the betrothal. The woman would continue to live at her parents' home for about a year, at least until puberty when she became capable of childbearing.

This state of betrothal was a legal relationship. If the man died during the period, the woman was considered a widow. In at least some parts of Judea, a sexual relationship between the two was acceptable. Some scholars believe that the social mores in Galilee where Joseph and Mary lived were stricter and that sexual intercourse during the betrothal was deemed improper. Whatever the approved practice, Matthew clearly asserts that Mary had not yet come to live with her husband and that they had had no sexual intercourse. Luke concurs, speaking of Mary as a virgin.

The Betrothal

This pattern of betrothal is supported in the Protevangelion. The angel announced to Mary that she would conceive "the Son of the Living God." As in Luke's narrative, Mary later visited Elizabeth, who greeted her as "the mother of my Lord." Mary returned home, at that time several months pregnant. "And [she] was fourteen years old when all these things happened" (Protevangelion 9:11-23)

Read Numbers 5:11-31, a test of adultery, and Deuteronomy 22:20-21, the punishment. Luke does not mention Joseph's distress at this pregnancy as Matthew does. Why do you suppose the angel did not reveal this pregnancy to Joseph earlier and save him the anguish? What were Joseph's options according to the law? What does his decision reveal about his character?

When Joseph learned that Mary was pregnant, he knew that the child could not be his. He surely must have assumed that his betrothed had been unfaithful to him. In the midst of the disappointment and anger that he must have felt, Joseph had to make a decision. The law was quite clear about his responsibility. Deuteronomy 22:20-21 prescribes the execution of such an adulterous woman by stoning. While he might have sought this option, a less strict interpretation of this law in Joseph's time offered him the choice of divorce instead. Joseph felt that he had to divorce Mary in order to obey the law, but he was a merciful man who was "unwilling to expose her to public disgrace." Probably this meant that Joseph was not willing publicly to accuse Mary of adultery— a charge that might have subjected her to trial in accord with Numbers 5:11-31. Righteous Joseph was also a kind man, a man of mercy, willing to be disgraced himself in order to avoid hurting his betrothed, even if she had sorely wronged him.

The words of the angel who appeared to Joseph at this point solved his dilemma. Since the pregnancy was "from the Holy Spirit," he would not be in violation of the law by taking Mary into his home as his wife. But it was not so easy as that, not in the world of real men and women.

Look at William Willimon's comment from *Christian Century*. What does it mean to you to "set out on a lonely, uncharted path" in order to be obedient to God's plans? Have you ever

In an Advent meditation, Will Willimon, writing in *Christian Century* (November 23, 1988) helps us to feel the confusion and pain of Joseph's situation:

---

felt called, even com-
pelled, to a course of
action by God that seemed
difficult and painful? What
was that experience like?
What did you do? Where
did you look for support?
Did you find it? Who have
been the "Josephs" in your
life?

"Mary may have been blessed among women, but righteous Joseph was embarrassed among men. . . . Few painters tried their hands at Matthew's annunciation: Joseph bolting upright in bed, in a cold sweat after the nightmare of being told that his fiancée is pregnant, and not by him, and that he should marry her anyway." In believing that Mary's child was divinely given, "Joseph set out on a lonely, uncharted path of marrying a pregnant fiancée and taking her child as his own, thus assuming responsibility for the child who, when called, answered [not to the name Joseph Jr., but] to Emmanuel [God With Us]."

Throughout the infancy stories, Joseph consistently behaved with integrity and courage. Interestingly, he never spoke throughout the narratives. Joseph was a man who expressed his faith in action. He obeyed the instructions and heeded the warnings sent from God. Dreams as a medium of God's word remind the reader of a much earlier namesake.

Instruments of God's Plan

Review the contributions to
our salvation history by
Zechariah, Elizabeth, and
Joseph. How would you
summarize what they did
and what they represented
to our faith and faith
history?

Joseph, son of Jacob, whose story is told in Genesis 37–50, also went into Egypt as an instrument of divine purpose. Jesus' father Joseph is not mentioned in any of the Gospel accounts beyond the time of the visit to the Temple when Jesus was twelve years old (Luke 2:41-51). Probably he had died before the beginning of Jesus' public ministry.

Both Matthew and Luke trace Jesus' descent from King David through Joseph. Both genealogies are versions of Joseph's ancestry. Yet both writers insist that Joseph was not the human father of Jesus. (Notice in Matthew 2:13-15 how carefully Matthew avoids calling Joseph Jesus' father.) Davidic descent was not determined by natural paternity but by a man's legal acknowledgment that the child was his. Joseph made this claim when he named Jesus—the legal father had the right to choose the child's name.

Three supporting actors—Zechariah, Elizabeth, and Joseph—were all righteous before God and used as God's instruments in the work of salvation. They were minor actors in the drama of the infancy narratives, but each played an essential role. Through Zechariah, the story of God's action for human salvation through the Hebrew people is linked to God's new work through Jesus Christ. Through Elizabeth is born the child whose ministry will be that of the divinely sent messenger who prepares the way for the coming of the Christ. Through Joseph the Christ is brought into the heritage of David. A just and merciful father claims and protects the Holy Child.

Closing Prayer ■

Zechariah, Elizabeth, and Joseph were invited in compelling ways into the "Jesus story." Consider for a moment how God may be calling you to a more intimate role in the community of faith. Take time either to make or to renew your commitment to God through Christ.

Close with your circle prayer and include prayers for all the unsung men and women of faith who have and who do offer themselves in extraordinary ways to the service of God.

Session Five

Foremothers of Faith

Session Focus

Mary, the mother of Jesus, has been the subject of both inquiry and adoration. In Roman Catholicism and Eastern Orthodoxy, Mary occupies a place of honor secondary only to that of Christ himself. Miracles are regularly attributed to her influence. Who was this young teenager who became the mother of God? What is her significance for Christian believers today?

Session Objective

We want to look carefully at what Scripture says about Mary's role in the coming of Christ. Controversy about the subject of the virgin birth and about Mary herself will not be resolved, but will be examined and analyzed especially for what it teaches about Jesus.

Session Preparation

Using a concordance, locate and read all of the references to Mary in the New Testament, or at least a selected portion of them from the four Gospels. (Be sure to distinguish Jesus'

Whereas Matthew's focus in his infancy narrative is on Joseph, Luke emphasizes the role of Mary. Both she and her relative Elizabeth, the mother of John the Baptist, call our attention to the role of women in the redemption of Israel at various points in its history. In the period of the judges, "Deborah, a prophetess, . . . was judging Israel. She used to sit under the palm of Deborah . . . and the Israelites came up to her for judgment" (Judges 4:4-5). When the people of Israel were suffering oppression by the Canaanites, Deborah called Barak and directed him to lead an army against them. Barak's response is surprising for a general in a very patriarchal society: "If you will go with me, I will go; but if you do not go with me, I will not go" (4:8).

At the end of the battle when the Israelites prevailed, the enemy general Sisera was killed by Jael, a woman in whose tent he had sought rest and shelter. Hoping to elude capture, he hid under a rug. Jael's action, while horrifying, illustrates an unusually powerful role for a woman among the Hebrews. Jael "took a tent peg, and took a hammer in her hand, and went softly to him and drove the peg into his temple, until it went down into the ground" (4:21). Deborah's song of triumph in Judges 5 is thought to be one of the oldest pieces of literature in the Hebrew Bible.

mother from the other Marys.)

If possible, invite a knowledgeable Roman Catholic to attend the session to help you understand the Catholic teachings about Mary. In addition, check your local or church library for art books that portray Mary in various artistic periods and styles.

Choose from among these activities and discussion starters to plan your lesson.

Foremothers of Faith ■

Read Judges 4–5 as a sample of both the cycle of apostasy and deliverance and of the contribution of one significant woman in the salvation history of Israel. What is the evidence in the story of God's providential work in Deborah? How do women figure in this story? What does this mean in a male-dominant society? to you? Why do you think the roles and contributions of women in both religious and secular history have been given such little attention? What do we lose when this happens over the decades?

Cycle of Apostasy and Deliverance

Throughout the Book of Judges, God raises up a number of deliverers as part of what scholars refer to as a cycle of apostasy and deliverance. The cycle begins with a time of peace and prosperity; God's presence and grace are evident in the life of Israel (see, for example, Judges 3:30).

At the next stage, complacency and divine forgetfulness emerge: Israel either forgets or takes for granted God's goodness and begins to fall into neglectful habits in their worship and social justice (see Judges 4:1). This descent into apostasy (worship of other deities) elicits God's wrath, and God allows a foreign power, such as King Jabin, to rise up and defeat Israel (4:2).

When Israel reflects on this sin and repents, God hears their plea for help (4:3) and raises up a charismatic leader to free Israel from that bondage (4:4-24). Under God's guidance and providence, the judge prevails, and Israel returns to a time of peace and prosperity (5:31)—until complacency sets in and the cycle begins again.

While the Book of Judges reveals this cycle in a very tidy way, the fall from righteousness and the need for deliverance are themes that permeate the Scriptures and bear continual witness to the need for a Savior.

The need for deliverance emerges in numerous books of the Bible. In the book that bears her name, Esther, a Jewish woman married to the Persian king, risked her own life to save her people from massacre. The Apocrypha contains the Book of Judith, the story of another Jewish heroine who must have emulated her ancestor Jael. Judith protected herself from rape by getting the

Assyrian general Holofernes "dead drunk." While he was sleeping, she "took down his sword that hung there. She came close to his bed, . . . and said, 'Give me strength today, O Lord God of Israel!' Then she struck his neck twice with all her might, and cut off his head" (Judith 13:2, 6b-8). Judith's action saved Jerusalem from the invading Assyrian army. Throughout Hebrew history countless other women, obedient and faithful to God, served in diverse ways as instruments of God's will. Unfortunately for the community of faith, their stories are often overlooked and forgotten.

Blessed Among Women

The Roman Catholic *Catechism* uses an intriguing statement about Mary's conception of Christ: "Mary was invited to conceive him. . . ." What might this mean about Mary?

Form three groups and divide among them the three Old Testament Annunciation stories. What are the elements in those stories? What happened at the Annunciation? What feelings or reactions did those persons who heard the heavenly message have? From what you remember of these Old Testament stories, what was the result? What does it have to do with the unfolding plan of our salvation history?

Blessed Among Women

Mary's name is another form of "Miriam"—the name of the sister of Moses who sang praise to God after the crossing of the sea (Exodus 15:20-21). As indicated in the last session, Mary was probably a young woman just entering her teens when she became the mother of the Christ Child. She lived in the town of Nazareth and was betrothed to Joseph. This is all the information that Luke gives us about Mary prior to the visit of the angel. Luke focuses the spotlight on Mary when the angel Gabriel visits her—the same messenger who had announced to Zechariah the impending birth of John the Baptist. The mention of "the sixth month" in Luke 1:26 refers to the pregnancy of Elizabeth. A part of Gabriel's revelation to Mary was to tell her of her kinswoman's blessing.

Luke 1:26-38 is the account of the Annunciation—the announcement to Mary of her pregnancy. Traditionally, it is celebrated by the church on March 25, a date determined simply by counting backward from December 25. Annunciation stories had

Now read Luke 1:26-38. Note the five stages. How does this Annunciation compare with the ones from the Hebrew Scriptures?

Imagine that an angel has appeared to tell you some startling but good news. What might be your emotional response? your practical response? What would your family and friends say to you if you told them about an angelic visitation? Do you think God could or would interact this way with us now? Explain.

Bible 301 ☐

Using the art books, study and discuss several paintings of the Annunciation. How is Mary characterized? What does the artistic rendering of this scene evoke from you? · How does it affect your faith or understanding of Mary's role?

developed into an almost stereotypical form in the Old Testament. We see the pattern, for example, in the announcement of the birth of Ishmael to the slave woman Hagar in Genesis 16:7-13; in the encounter of Abraham and Sarah with the angel who tells them of the birth of Isaac in Genesis 18:10-15; and perhaps most clearly in the announcement to Samson's parents in Judges 13:3-23. Luke uses this form in relating Gabriel's announcement to Zechariah.

The pattern of annunciation has five parts: (1) the appearance of an angel as a messenger to someone who is to play a significant role in the divine plan, (2) the response of fear, (3) the delivery of the divine message, (4) the objection or questioning of the message, and (5) the giving of a sign as a guarantee. In Luke 1:28, Gabriel appears to Mary and addresses her. The older translation of his greeting included "full of grace." Many scholars, certainly most Protestant ones, believe this to be a misleading translation since it may imply some special quality possessed by Mary herself. Instead, it is the divine favor that has chosen her that makes her special. Verses 32-33 are a loose restatement of God's promises to David in 2 Samuel 7:8-16. Mary's child is to be the hoped-for king of the lineage of David. After being told about Elizabeth's pregnancy as the sign or guarantee, Mary responds in a way that is not a part of the usual annunciation pattern. In Luke 1:38, she obediently accepts the role given to her by God. This verse is an indicator of how Luke will portray Mary in the remainder of his Gospel. Unlike as in Mark, Mary and others in Jesus' human family become his disciples; they do not reject him (compare Mark 3:31-35 and Luke 8:19-21).

"How Can This Be?"

The angel announced an unorthodox conception process. Review Luke 1:26-38 and Matthew 1:18-25 and compare the activity of the angel in the two stories. Who did the angel speak to? What was said? What was the emotional response? the practical response?

How would you explain this conception story to someone from a religious tradition that has no common roots with Christianity? How did God do what the angel said would happen?

"How Can This Be?"

The most striking part of Gabriel's announcement to Mary is in Luke 1:35: "The Holy Spirit will come upon you, and the power of the Most High will overshadow you; therefore the child to be born will be holy; he will be called Son of God." It is only in this annunciation account (1:26-38) and in Matthew 1:18-25 that there is any reference to Mary's virginity. Elsewhere throughout the New Testament, Jesus is assumed to be the biological child of his legal father Joseph. This may raise questions, but it does not necessarily diminish the significance of this "doctrine of the virgin birth." Actually the more appropriate term here is the "virginal conception" it is the conception of Jesus in Mary's womb that is being explained, not Mary's virginity at the time of his birth.

In Matthew's somewhat-less-dramatic account, this information is given to Joseph. Matthew substantiates the virginal conception through the use of the first of his formula quotations from the Old Testament. Matthew 1:23 quotes "what had been spoken by the Lord, through the prophet: / 'Look, the virgin shall conceive and bear a son, / and they shall name him Emmanuel,' / which means 'God is with us.'" These words are from Isaiah 7:14.

"I Am a Virgin"

Compare Isaiah 7:14 with other passages that are considered Messianic references: Isaiah 9:2-7; 11:1-5; Matthew 1:20-23; Luke 1:30-35. Is conception to a virgin stated or implied in all of them? How are the characteristics of the Messiah similar or different?

"I Am a Virgin"

In the New Revised Standard Version, and in many other English translations, the Isaiah verse reads: "Therefore the Lord himself will give you a sign. Look, the young woman is with child and shall bear a son, and shall name him Immanuel." The Hebrew word *almah* is usually translated as "young woman." Matthew used the Septuagint, a Greek translation of the Old Testament, in

The belief in the literal virgin birth of Christ has been
debated for centuries and
is part of our historic
creeds. Look up the
Apostles' Creed, the
Nicene Creed, and other
affirmations of faith in your
worship resources. Is a
statement of belief in the
virgin birth a part of all of
them? Do you think it is
essential to the Christian
faith? to your faith?
Explain.

which that Hebrew term is translated into the Greek word *parthenos,* meaning "virgin."

This is an unusual translation of the verse and appears in almost no modern version of the Bible. Jewish scholars assert that there are no similar uses in Jewish writings and that there was no expectation of a messiah who would be born of a virgin.

In its original form, Isaiah 7:14 probably was a part of the prophet's reassurance to King Ahaz that Judah would be protected by God from the military threat it faced. The kings of the Northern Kingdom of Israel and of Syria were pressuring Ahaz to join them against the might of Assyria. Isaiah assures the king that there is no need to join such an alliance. Indeed, it would be folly to do so. God will not allow the conquest of Judah at this time. Judah's deliverance would occur soon, before a certain (unknown) pregnant woman gave birth.

Matthew is not constrained in his use of the Isaiah text, although he must have known its meaning in its original context. He understood Jesus Christ to be the fulfill-ment of all Scripture.

Isaiah 7:14 is a controversial verse among Christians even today. In 1952, when the Old Testament portion of the Revised Standard Version of the Bible was published, it was vilified and even burned by some Christian groups because it used the term "young woman" instead of "virgin." The Roman Catholic translators of what became the New American Bible (1972) reluctantly used the term "virgin" only when forced to by the American bishops. Controversy relat-ed to the issue is not limited to questions of appropriate translation.

The historical facticity of what is called the virgin birth has been and continues to be a subject of debate among Christians. In the fundamentalist movement that attained great strength in Protestant churches in the 1920's, one of the five essential points of doctrine was the virgin birth. There are still many who use this issue as a test of the orthodoxy of other Christians.

A Legitimate Child

On the other hand, most Christian scholars today, even those who would be considered conservative, are not insisting on agreement about historical fact. Yet, in the vast majority of churches, congregations very often (many weekly) recite the Apostles' Creed with its affirmation that Christ was "born of the Virgin Mary." Intentional teaching by clergy and other church leaders is imperative if Christian people are to be able to appreciate the significance of Matthew and Luke's accounts of virginal conception in our understanding of the person of Jesus Christ. Obviously, the significance of this doctrine goes far beyond the Isaiah verse, regardless of its translation or meaning. At the least, both Matthew and Luke knew and used a tradition that the birth of Jesus was in some way unusual.

Some scholars believe that the accounts represent the effort of the early Christian church to counter rumors and charges that Jesus was an illegitimate child. Such rumors were in existence by the mid-second century. In the second century the philosopher Celsus made the charge of illegitimacy (among other things) in his debate with the Christian philosopher Origen. Possibly this suspicion is being hinted at earlier in Mark 6:3. It is doubtful that the Gospel writers would have made up the story of virginal conception, since it would attract charges of illegitimacy.

When you participate in reciting one of the "virgin birth" creeds, what goes through your mind? If we do not believe in any portion of a creed, do we abrogate belief in other portions of that creed? Does unbelief in a portion of a creed somehow undermine our faith or doctrine? Explain.

The Divine
and Human Child ■

One might suppose that Mary's child, who was not biologically from Joseph, could be branded as illegitimate. Celsus not only leveled those charges but also suggested that the child was the son of a poor seamstress and a soldier named Panthera. Origen wrote eight books to refute him. What does it mean to you that Jesus was "conceived by the Holy Spirit"? How can Jesus be divine and human at the same time? What does this mean to you?

For Matthew and Luke, Jesus became the divine Christ at the moment of his conception. Could this have happened any other way? Explain.

Treasured
in Her Heart ■

Look up the three passages in which Mary "treasured in her heart" some activity of God: Luke 1:29, 2:19, 2:51, and a few surrounding verses. What might Mary have been thinking and feeling as she experienced these extraordinary events? Do you think she understood fully what was going on and what would eventually happen? Does it make any difference? Why or why not?

The Divine and Human Child

The account of Jesus' conception is quite different from myths in other cultures in which gods mate with human women and produce demigod offspring. In neither Matthew nor Luke is there any implication that the Holy Spirit functioned in the male role of the reproductive act. The "overshadowing" by "the power of the Most High" (Luke 1:35) is not described as a sexual action. It is the creative power of the Holy Spirit that is at work, similar to the divine work in Genesis 1:1-2. It is the same as the resurrection power by which Christ was raised from the dead. (See Romans 1:3-4 and 8:11.) Here is God taking the initiative in a way far beyond the capacity of mortals to understand, to bring divinity into the vessel of a human mother's womb.

The point of the story is that the child Mary has conceived is unique. He is the child of God in a way that far exceeds the meaning of that phrase as it is applied to other human beings. For Matthew and Luke, Jesus of Nazareth became the divine Christ at the moment of his conception.

Treasured in Her Heart

Not only in the Annunciation account, but at least twice more in Luke's infancy narrative, the reader is allowed tiny glimpses into the mind and heart of Mary. After the visit of the shepherds who told about their encounter with the angelic hosts of heaven, Luke notes, "But Mary treasured all these words and pondered them in her heart" (2:19). Twelve years later, when Jesus' worried parents have found him in the Temple and heard him say that he must be in his Father's house, "his mother treasured all these things in her heart" (2:51b). What must this young mother have thought as she experienced the strange events surrounding her beloved son's birth and childhood? How much did she understand? What must she have felt—joy, confusion, fear?

The "Mother of God"

The "Mother of God"

If you invited a Roman Catholic guest, ask him or her to lead the discussion about the doctrine of Immaculate Conception, which refers to Mary's conception, not to that of Jesus. What does it state? Does her immaculate conception make a difference in her role as the future mother of Jesus? If Jesus was acquainted with sin and temptation (though without sin) to better identify with the sin of humankind, is it necessary that Mary should also be immune from original sin? Would it be important or necessary for a mother to be preserved from original sin in order to bear and rear a divine son? Explain your responses.

Now, with your guest if possible, examine the doctrine of Perpetual Virginity. What is it?

The virgin Mary has, of course, figured far more prominently in Roman Catholic belief and practice than in that of Protestants. While Protestants surely do not have to accept all Roman Catholic teachings, it is wise to be informed about them. Perhaps also, a fuller study of Mary might enhance the appreciation of the role she played in God's supreme act of salvation.

Tradition claims that Mary was the daughter of Joachim and Anne—an elderly couple who were childless before her birth. The doctrine of the Immaculate Conception has its earliest traditions in the second century. The feast of her conception was first known in the seventh century, though the doctrine was not made official church dogma until 1854. It is often confused with that of the virgin birth.

The Immaculate Conception has nothing directly to do with the conception of Jesus. Instead, it refers to the conception of his mother Mary. The Bull *Ineffabilis Deus* of Pope Pius IX, December 8, 1854, states that "from the first moment of her conception the Blessed Virgin Mary was, by the singular grace and privilege of Almighty God and in view of the merits of Jesus Christ, Savior of mankind, kept free from all stain of original sin."

Since sexual activity is closely associated with sin, all human beings are born into this world bearing a sinful nature. Not so for Mary, according to the Catholic catechism.

Read Matthew 12:46-50; Mark 3:31-35, 6:3; Luke 8:19-21; John 7:3-5; Acts 1:14; and Galatians 1:19, which refer to Jesus' family members. If these persons were cousins or close family friends or considered family by virtue of being fellow believers, would this fact influence your faith or belief? your understanding of Scripture?

By a special intervention of God, Mary was sanctified and preserved from sin from her mother's womb. This was necessary in order for her to be qualified to serve as the mother of Christ.

The doctrine of the Perpetual Virginity of Mary is another point on which Roman Catholic and Protestant teaching diverge. According to the Gospel accounts, Mary lived throughout the ministry of Jesus and would probably have been in her late forties when he was crucified. Joseph had almost surely died earlier. Catholicism teaches that Mary remained a virgin throughout her lifetime. The birth of Jesus did not alter her physical state of virginity, and she bore no other children. As stated in *Catechism of the Catholic Church* (Image, Doubleday, 1995): "The deepening of faith in the virginal motherhood led the Church to confess Mary's real and perpetual virginity even in the act of giving birth to the Son of God made man. . . . And so the liturgy of the Church celebrates Mary as *Aeiparthenos*, the 'Ever-virgin.'"

Read three Ascension stories: Acts 1:1-11; 2 Kings 2:1-12; and Genesis 5:23-24. The doctrine of the Bodily Assumption of Mary places her in the company of Enoch, Elijah, and Jesus (although Jesus paradoxically died physically first, was resurrected, and then was raised later after "presenting himself alive" to the disciples). What is the meaning of these Ascension stories? What does it say about the life and importance of the person who was "taken up"? Does belief (or not) in Mary's assumption affect

This idea became common teaching toward the end of the fourth century. Of course, it immediately raises the question of the four brothers and an unknown number of sisters of Jesus who are mentioned in the New Testament. Catholicism claims that these were not Mary's offspring, but rather cousins of Jesus or children of Joseph by a previous marriage. Interestingly, even Martin Luther and John Calvin, two outstanding leaders in the breakaway from Rome, also taught that these "brothers and sisters" were instead cousins of Jesus.

Another much earlier doctrine, which was only declared official dogma in 1950, is that of the Bodily Assumption of Mary. The

your faith? your under-
standing of Mary?

Catechism teaches that: "Finally the Immaculate Virgin, preserved free from all stain of original sin, when the course of her earthly life was finished, was taken up body and soul into heavenly glory, and exalted by the Lord as Queen over all things, so that she might be more fully conformed to her Son."

The Queen of Heaven ■

Several other titles or attributes of Mary are "advocate, helper, benefactress, and mediatrix." What would it mean to Protestants to have another mediator in addition to Jesus Christ? How does Mary advocate or help? Does this doctrine mean that Mary is on the same level of mercy as God or on an equal par in salvation as Jesus Christ?

The Queen of Heaven

The use of "Queen" in the previous quotation is foreign to Protestants, but very common to Roman Catholics who often refer to Mary as the Queen of Heaven. In modern Catholicism there is an undeniable tendency to think and speak of Mary as Co-redemptrix—as sharing with Christ in the work of redeeming the world. The new *Catechism* states, "Therefore the Blessed Virgin is invoked in the Church under the titles of Advocate, Helper, Benefactress, and Mediatrix."

The idea is that Mary, being fully human and without the benefit of a divine nature, can identify with and pity us in our sin and intercede with Christ for our forgiveness: "You conceived the living God and, by your prayers, will deliver our souls from death" (*Catechism*). These teachings are not only foreign to Protestants but also problematic. Mary must not be portrayed as being more merciful than God, as more inclined to forgive and aid Christians than is Christ.

Pope John Paul II is especially devoted to the Blessed Virgin and speaks of her often in his worldwide travels. The period of his papacy, since 1978, has been characterized by a resurgence of attention to Mary and the various devotional practices and beliefs associated with her. This Polish pope is surely influenced by the tradition of the Black

Madonna, a shrine associated with Polish nationalism.

Perhaps most famous is the shrine at Lourdes in southwestern France where pilgrims come, many seeking healing. In 1858, a young French girl, who was later canonized, saw eighteen apparitions of Mary there. Lourdes is visited by millions of persons every year.

Mary and Contemporary Protestant Christians

It might be thought that reverence for the virgin Mary would have magnified the role and elevated the status of women in the church. This, however, has not been the case. Throughout the history of the Christian church, women have been subjugated to male authority and considered inferior to men. Often the association of women with sin has supported this situation. For example, Tertullian, an influential Christian thinker, wrote (about A.D. 200) to women: "*You* are the devil's gateway: *you* are the unsealer of that (forbidden) tree: . . . *You* destroyed so easily God's image, man. . . . On account of *your* desert—that is, death—even the Son of God had to die" ("On the Apparel of Women" quoted in *Readings in Her Story: Women in the Christian Tradition*, edited by Barbara J. MacHaffie, Fortress Press, 1992).

While Tertullian's charges are obviously extreme, it cannot be denied that the church has not, and in many ways does not yet, encourage the fullest development of women's gifts. Despite Mary's service as mediator and intercessor, Roman Catholicism still refuses to ordain women to the priesthood. While most mainline Protestant denominations do now have women pastors, opposition still exists; and discrimination is

---

Mary and Protestants ■

Summarize the Roman Catholic views of Mary and compare them with your understanding of the Scriptures in this session and the views of your church. What could we learn from each other's beliefs? What are the benefits of the veneration of Mary? What are the dangers?

In Judaism and Christianity God has traditionally been thought and spoken of in male terms. When Christians think seriously about this, most will acknowledge that God is not actually male as opposed to female. Recognizing that God transcends human gender distinctions, how can the faith expand the idea of God to include all that it means to be male and female? Is it important to do this? Why or why not? Can Mary, the mother of Jesus, contribute anything to this idea?

---

not unusual. Issues of the appropriate roles for men and women in the church and in the larger society continue today. Mary sets a standard for womanhood that is impossible to meet; no woman can attain her status. The virgin Mother is ideal and unique.

What Honor Is Due?

What then can Mary mean for Protestant Christians? She can be honored as a person who gave her life to God, who cooperated with the divine purpose, and is an exemplar to the church of obedience and self-giving. In the infancy narratives, Mary represents the continuity between God's saving acts in the history of Israel and God's supreme act of salvation in the person and work of Christ. She is a sign of God's decisive intervention in human history, a signpost pointing to Christ. A contemporary collect in *The Book of Common Prayer* (Kingsport Press, 1977) seems to express at least a bit of how Mary can be honored by Protestants:

"Father in heaven, by your grace the virgin mother of thy incarnate Son was blessed in bearing him, but still more blessed in keeping thy word: Grant us who honor the exaltation of her lowliness to follow the example of her devotion to thy will; through the same Jesus Christ our Lord, who liveth and reigneth with thee and the Holy Spirit, one God, for ever and ever."

What Honor Is Due? ■

If the status and role of Mary, at least in the Catholic tradition, is unattainable, how can Mary be a model of faithfulness for contemporary Christians? If you are a man, can you relate at all to Mary's place in our salvation history? If so, how? What about her life do you find inspiring? What do you find that is worth emulating?

Closing Prayer ■

Mary invested her life in Jesus. Her experience beckons us to invest ourselves as well. Take time in prayer to consider your relationship to Jesus Christ and to make or reaffirm your commitment.

Close with your circle prayers, including prayer for those who struggle to know God more intimately.

Session Six

Shepherds and Angels, Wise Men and a Star

Session Focus ■

This session will look at the story of the shepherds told in Luke's Gospel and the story of the wise men or magi recounted in Matthew. We will distinguish what is actually recorded in the biblical record from the myriad of traditions that Christians over the centuries have added. More significantly, we will focus on how these persons responded to the good news of Christ's birth and how we as present-day Christians should respond.

Session Objective ■

The birth of Christ is good news to and for all persons. It is, however, those who are dispossessed, suffering, and discriminated against who can help us to appreciate the gospel more fully.

Session Preparation ■

Read carefully the account of the shepherds in Luke 2:8-20 and that of the wise men in Matthew 2:1-12. Bring a Bible concordance.

Let us review the order of events associated with the birth of Christ as they are told in the Gospel according to Luke. The first character to be introduced is Zechariah. We learn about his encounter in the Temple with the angel Gabriel who tells the incredulous priest that he is to be the father of John the Baptist. Next comes the Annunciation to Mary when she is told that, her virginity not withstanding, she will be the mother of the Christ. Mary travels to the home of her kinswoman Elizabeth, the wife of Zechariah. The two women recognize the mighty work that God is doing through their unexpected pregnancies and the sons that they will bear.

Mary praises God in a beautiful canticle called the Magnificat, to be discussed further in the next chapter. After Mary returns to Nazareth, Elizabeth gives birth to the child who is named John. His father Zechariah recovers his ability to speak and praises God in the canticle we refer to as the Benedictus. The second chapter of Luke opens with the census decree that necessitates Mary and Joseph's journey to Bethlehem. While they are there, Jesus is born.

Meet the Shepherds

Immediately Luke moves to the account of the shepherds to whom the angel brings news of this momentous birth. It is not surprising

Shepherds and Angels ■

Using the chart begun in previous sessions, continue to list in separate columns the events told in the infancy narratives of Matthew and Luke. Review the birth and pre-birth gospel narrative that you have covered to this point as a review.

Meet the Shepherds ■

Read Luke 2:8-12. Briefly recall what you know about biblical shepherds. If anyone in the group has cared for sheep, invite him or her to describe the responsibilities that shepherding entails.

The Shepherd in Hebrew Scripture ■

Look up Psalm 23 and Micah 5:2-5. How is the good shepherd portrayed? How does the metaphor of the good shepherd serve to assure and encourage people who struggle? What are the implements that the shepherd in Psalm 23 carries, and how do they serve as instruments of care?

that Luke focuses so much on events involving the shepherds. One of the characteristics of his Gospel is the emphasis upon groups of people who are poor, oppressed, and otherwise marginalized.

Shepherds had low status in Palestinian society. They even may have been despised because of their reputation for dishonesty. It is to these lowly people that the good news of Christ's birth is first announced. The ordinary people of the land were suffering from poverty and oppression. They were looking to God to deliver them. They were straining to hear the good news that the angel would proclaim.

Dumb but Useful

Sheep are dumb animals, which makes them particularly vulnerable; they depend heavily on the shepherd for their safety. Nevertheless, they were the most important domestic animals in Palestine. Nearly everyone in ancient Palestine had some involvement with sheep. With their economic importance, even villagers and townspeople were likely to keep some sheep. Not only were sheep a principle sacrificial animal, they provided meat, milk, fat, wool, skins, and horns.

The Shepherd in Hebrew Scripture

Jesus would doubtless have been familiar with Psalm 23, which likens God to the good shepherd who cares for every need of the sheep for safety, sustenance, and comfort. Shepherding may have been considered menial work, but a good shepherd had to be patient, diligent, and enduring. Searching for lost sheep, enduring all kinds of weather, and traveling wherever there was pasture and

How does Micah character-
ize the good shepherd?

Now contrast these images
with Ezekiel 34. What can
you tell by inference about
the rulers of Israel? What
happens when the shep-
herd does not do his job
properly?

What image might we sub-
stitute for "shepherd" in
an urban setting today?
How might persons today
who do not relate to rural
or agrarian images under-
stand the place of the
shepherd in biblical
Palestine and thus the
place of this image for our
faith today?

Jesus and Shepherding ■

Form three groups and
divide among them the
passages on sheep and
shepherds in Luke 15,
Matthew 15, and John 10.
Be sure each small-group
member understands the
passage, then rewrite it in
terms that seem to make
sense in the type of setting
(rural, suburban, or urban)
in which you live. What difference does this new
image make in how you
might hear the message
directly from Jesus in your
own context?

water was hard work. Thieves and wild animals might strike the shepherd as well as the
sheep. Were it not for the shepherd's staff
and rod, they were essentially unprotected.

Jesus was of the lineage of David, probably
to us the most important shepherd ever
mentioned in the Hebrew Scriptures. All of
the patriarchs were shepherds, and quite
prosperous as a result. Jesus would have also
been aware of the prophetic imagery that
compared kings and other rulers of Israel to
shepherds.

In Ezekiel 34 we read of the bitter com-
plaints that Israel's leaders have abandoned
their "flock" just as a poor shepherd might
run off and leave the sheep in danger of
predators. Micah 5:2-5a was the prophetic
word that was understood to indicate that
the birth of the Messiah would be in
Bethlehem. It is significant that verse 4
describes him as a shepherd ruler: "And he
shall stand and feed his flock in the strength
of the LORD, / in the majesty of the name of
the LORD his God."

Jesus and Shepherding

Often in the Gospels Jesus is identified with
the role of a shepherd. Best known is perhaps
Luke's parable of the good shepherd in 15:3-7
and Jesus' description of himself as a good
shepherd and as the door of the sheep gate in
John 10. He also lamented that those who fol-
lowed him hungering for every good word
were as sheep without a shepherd. Matthew
reports that Jesus spoke of himself as coming
to "the lost sheep of the house of Israel"
(Matthew 15:24) as the good shepherd who
cared intimately about the pain and misery of
humankind, for their well-being. It is not at
all unusual that Luke would have reported the
angelic visit to the shepherds in Bethlehem.

Shepherds and Angels, Wise Men and a Star **77**

The Shepherds Visited by Angels

Why do you think God chose these shepherds as the first to hear the good news of the birth of God's Holy Child? What does this divine choice tell us about God?

Imagine yourself at your ordinary daily activities, experiencing the sudden appearance of angels who speak and sing to you. Divide into clusters of three to share your thoughts. Is there a sense in which the angels sent from God are continuing to proclaim the good news today? Why is it so hard for us to hear the angels' song? Is it easier or harder to hear it at Christmastime? Explain.

In the hymnal used by your congregation, find and read or sing some of the many Christmas carols that feature the shepherds and the angels. Probably the most widely used are "It Came upon a Midnight Clear," "Hark! the Herald Angels Sing," "While Shepherds Watched Their Flocks," and "Angels We Have Heard on High." What are some insights that can be gleaned from these carols?

Savior, Messiah, and Lord

Refer again to Luke 2:10-14 and read Isaiah 19:20 and 43:3. Form three groups. Ask each one to focus on a different title that angels proclaim for the newborn child—Savior, Messiah, and Lord. What is

The Shepherds Visited by Angels

The shepherds and their flocks are in the open country outside Bethlehem. Because of this fact, some scholars have argued that the time of the birth must have been between March and November, when weather allowed the flocks to be kept outside to pasture. The flocks used for sacrifices in the Temple were probably kept nearby throughout the year.

The area today called the Shepherds' Fields is about two miles from Jerusalem toward the Dead Sea, below the snow line. The angel's appearance to the shepherds at night is the only indication that the birth occurred at that time. Perhaps Luke was influenced by a lovely passage from the apocryphal book, the Wisdom of Solomon, written in Greek only a few decades earlier: "For while gentle silence enveloped all things, / and night in its swift course was now half gone, / your all-powerful word leaped from heaven, from the royal throne" (18:14-15a).

When the angel comes to them, the shepherds respond as do most Bible characters in other situations: They are afraid. Terrified but attentive, they are the first to hear the announcement of the gospel—the good news of the coming of Christ. This is not some distant event, remote from their ordinary lives. The heavenly messenger specifically says that the child is born "to you." Great joy is granted to all who will receive it.

Savior, Messiah, and Lord

Luke casts the angelic proclamation in the form of an imperial edict, such as would have been read aloud by a herald. The angel calls the newborn child "a Savior, who is the Messiah, the Lord" (Luke 2:11). These three terms are important in understanding the person and work of Christ.

Savior is a term used only twice in Luke—both within the infancy narratives—and not at all by the other Synoptic writers. In the Old Testament it is used both for God and for the one God will send. (See Isaiah 19:20 and 43:3.) The child of whom the angel speaks will rescue and deliver the people—both from their sins and from their oppression. The child is also called the Messiah—the promised one sent from God to bring redemption.

This newborn is also "the Lord." In the Old Testament, the sacred name of God had been revealed to Moses in his encounter with the deity experienced in the burning bush (see Exodus 3). This divine name can best be translated from Hebrew with the English consonants YHWH. (Biblical Hebrew was written only in consonants, no vowels.) It was probably pronounced "Yahweh" and is the basis of further translation into "Jehovah." This name was considered by the Hebrews to be so sacred that it was not to be spoken aloud. The translators of the New Revised Standard Version of the Bible, as well as other translations, conform to the practice in ancient Jewish synagogues and substitute the word *LORD*, written in capital letters in order to indicate its meaning.

Applying this name to Jesus affirms that he is divine. A sign accompanies the proclamation, as is common when angels speak to humans. The baby will be found wrapped in bands of cloths, as was customary for Jewish infants. Much less common, he will be in a manger—a feed trough for animals. Is there a play here on the idea of God's sustenance and provision for God's people?

An Announcement

Refer again to Luke 2:13-14. Consider what is meant by the peace that God

An Announcement in Song

The startled shepherds' mouths and eyes must have opened even wider when the angel is joined by a host of heavenly singers glorifying and praising God (Luke 2:13-14). This brief hymn is known, by the Latin translation of its opening words, as the "Gloria in Excelsis Deo." Jewish literature in the period between the Old and New Testament often referred to multitudes of angels and many ascending levels of heaven. God is, of course, "in the highest heaven."

The gift of peace "among those [God] favors" raises questions. Who does God favor? Does not God favor or love all persons equally? Perhaps what Luke is implying is that God's peace can only come to those who will accept it. Those who believe and obey are those God favors, not because they deserve anything from God, but because they are willing to receive from God. While the coming of Christ brings great joy meant for all people, there are those such as Herod who will not receive it.

The shepherds do receive it. They believe and obey, going immediately to Bethlehem to see the child whose birth is so portentous that it was announced by angel heralds. The shepherds are, in a sense, the first disciples, perhaps the first evangelists. Their example challenges all Christians.

Power and Possibility to the Poor

I am further reminded of the power of the Christian gospel expressed in and through the base communities in Latin America in our own time. Faithful priests and teachers have recognized anew that God does indeed have a "preferential option" for the poor. Groups of poor peasants, politically and economically oppressed by the power structures of their society, are reading the Bible for themselves. They read with very different eyes than do comfortable middle-class

promises through Jesus Christ. (Note what Paul says in Philippians 4:4-7.) Use a concordance to find other references to "peace" in the New Testament.

Bible 301 ☐

Using a concordance, find "shepherd" and look up several references in the Bible. How often is the figure of a shepherd used for "God" and for "Christ"? How often does Jesus refer to himself or to Israel as sheep and shepherd? How often do the prophets announce the restoration of Israel or Jerusalem using a shepherding image?

Look up these key words (Savior, Messiah, Lord) in a concordance and Bible dictionary. What more does this information tell you about the person and role of Jesus Christ?

Power and Possibility to the Poor ■

Imagine, or tap into your own experience, a situation of real oppression (not just inconvenience or a single instance of injustice). Then read the angel's announcement again. Does it take on greater significance? For example, how might former slaves have heard this passage? current-day Christians in Muslim nations? persons who are regularly denied personal rights for whatever reason? refugees all over the world who are fleeing genocide?

Are you part of the unjust system? How can you be God's instrument in overturning human systems that perpetuate injustice and oppression?

The First Epiphany ■

What does *epiphany* mean? Read the two passages of Scripture associated with the themes of the Epiphany: Matthew 2:1-12 and Matthew 3:13-17. (Focus on Matthew 2:10-11 for this segment. The rest of the story of the magi will come later.) What are the similarities between these two passages? In what way are they epiphanies?

Have you ever had an experience in which God was suddenly made manifest and you could only stand in awe? What do you think it meant to Mary and Joseph to have these strange men come from such a long distance to pay

Christian Americans from the United States.

They hear and relate to the message of God's love for those who are marginalized. They perceive the revolutionary power of the biblical message that promises the overturning of human systems that seek to perpetuate the poverty of many in order to protect the wealth of few.

The First Epiphany

The story of the wise men, or *magi* from Latin, is told only in Matthew. These persons are not mentioned later in the Gospel or elsewhere in the New Testament. They play a significant part, however, in the drama of events around the birth of Jesus. The magi represent the non-Jewish world; they are foreigners drawn to the Christ Child who brings salvation for Jews and Gentiles alike. This is why the Christian church through the centuries and today celebrates the arrival of the magi in connection with the church year season of Epiphany.

The day of Epiphany is January 6—apparently the time when Jesus' birth was first celebrated. The celebration was moved to December 25 in the third century to counter the pagan festivals celebrated at the time of the winter solstice. Both January 6 and December 25 are days on which the Nativity is celebrated, depending on religious custom.

Christmastide and Epiphany

In Protestant traditions, Christmas celebrates the Nativity in a church season identified as Christmastide, which lasts twelve days, including Christmas Day. (Remember the partridge in the pear tree and all the other gifts?) The thirteenth day is recognized as the Day of Epiphany, January 6. Two epiphanies are cele-

homage to their son? In our culture, the advent of Christmas is marked commercially by how many shopping days are left before December 25. Many Christians are glad, on December 26, that Christmas is over, when religiously it has only just begun. How do you observe Advent (which generally begins the last Sunday of November), Christmastide, and Epiphany?

The Appearance of the Magi

Quickly recall whatever you can about the magi. What are *magi?* Where did they come from? How many were there? (Be brief; there will be more on this subject later.)

What Sort of Wisdom . . . ?

Read Numbers 22–24 for some background on the expectation that a star would figure in the Messiah's story. How is Matthew (2:1-6) likening Herod to Balak?

Herod was so cruel that if he were frightened, it would be natural for all of Jerusalem to fear as well— and so they should. See Matthew 2:13-18. How did

brated that day: the visit of the Gentiles who proclaimed the birth of the Messiah and the baptism of Jesus, when God proclaimed the sonship of Jesus

Epiphany means "manifestation" and is the season of emphasis upon the spread of the gospel throughout the world. The significance of the wise men is that they are the first non-Jews to whom the birth of Jesus is revealed. They are outsiders, but the coming of Christ is for all.

The Appearance of the Magi

Matthew tells little about these travelers from afar. As Matthew presents them, they are admirable characters, not charlatans or practitioners of evil arts (Matthew 2:1-12). They represent the best of the pagan world. Their careful study of the nighttime sky was to seek signs of divine will. In the appearance of a strange star, they saw a portent of the birth of one so significant that they were determined to find him. By the behavior of this star, they were guided to the place where this momentous event occurred.

What Sort of Wisdom Follows a Star?

The star of Bethlehem has been the subject of much speculation and many theories. Those who understand its appearance to have been an actual historical event have suggested various explanations—a supernova, a comet, a juxtaposition of planets. These theories, however, do not explain the supranatural movement of the star that guided these magi from the East. To bring them to Bethlehem, the star would first have gone westward, then southwestward, then "stood still." No scientific or historical certainty

God intervene on behalf of
the Holy Family?

exists. In the ancient world, new stars were believed to mark the births of great rulers or conquerors, such as Alexander the Great, for example.

Have you ever had the wisdom (or perhaps folly) to
symbolically "follow a star"
to someplace strange, new,
and promising? What was
that experience like? If you
had known ahead of time
what you later found out,
would you have done what
you did? Explain.

There was a traditional association in Judaism between the Messiah and a star. The rebel leader who led the Jews in their final revolt against Rome in A.D. 132–35 was called "Bar Cochba"—"the Star." The Old Testament background is found in Numbers 22–24, which is the story of Balak, king of Moab, and Balaam, a prophet of God. In his final oracle, Balaam declared, "I see him, but not now; / I behold him, but not near / a star shall come out of Jacob, / and a scepter shall rise out of Israel" (Numbers 24:17).

In accord with his theme of a conflict of kingdoms, Matthew likens King Herod to Balak. As an enemy ruler long ago sought to destroy Israel and was thwarted by God, so the tyrant who seeks to kill the newborn king of the Jews will likewise rage in vain.

The Gifts

The Gifts

What are the gifts and
what is their significance?
Perhaps the best-known
Christmas carol about the
magi is "We Three Kings."
Read the text noticing particularly what is said about
each of the gifts.

What do you suppose
Joseph and Mary did with
those gifts? (No one knows;
just use your imagination.)

This gift-giving is surely
one of the reasons we give
gifts at Christmas. In what
way do the gifts you select
and give honor the recipi-
ent? honor the Christ
Child? What personal

The gifts brought by the wise men to the Christ Child are significant. Gold was of great value and associated with kingship, especially the wealthy King Solomon, as in 1 Kings 10:2, 25. Frankincense and myrrh are both precious sweet-smelling gum resins, neither native to Palestine. By the fourth century, the Christian church had begun to elaborate the meaning of the gifts.

Gold symbolized virtue, assumedly for its purity. Frankincense, often burned in worship, symbolized prayer. Myrrh, used in anointing oil and in burials (as in John 19:39), was associated with suffering. It is only the number of gifts that suggests anything about the number of persons who were in the group: "three gifts equal three wise

investment and thought goes into your gift decisions? Do you see it as a pleasure or do you feel some other way? Explain.

Who Are the Magi? ▓

Using poster paper, make two lists—one of what the Matthean account actually tells us about the wise men or magi, another of some of the traditions that have developed around this story. (Recall your exercise with "The Appearance of the Magi.") While knowing these facts is perhaps more interesting than important, it is very important to recognize that too often we read the Bible through our own presuppositions and values. How can we learn to grasp what the biblical witness actually says, as opposed to what we assume it says or want it to say?

Look again at the list of traditional elements that have been added to the story. Explore what significance these traditions might have. Why do you think each one developed?

Read Psalm 72:10-11 and Isaiah 60:3-6. Using a map in your study Bible, locate Persia, Babylon, and Arabia. How far would the magi have to have traveled from each of these regions? Why do you think they undertook such a long and arduous journey? What was the impelling motivation?

men" has been the church's traditional assumption. Art found in the Roman catacombs, however, pictures various numbers of magi—two, four, and even twelve.

Who Are the Magi?

The story of the magi has aroused much curiosity and received considerable embellishment through the centuries. Nothing in the account indicates that these men were kings, as they are usually portrayed in Nativity scenes. Most likely, they were astrologers, with perhaps some magic, fortunetelling, and other occult arts thrown in. They may have been members of a priestly caste in Persia or Babylon, experts in interpreting dreams and natural phenomena. They came from the East, if not Persia or Babylon, then perhaps Arabia.

Quite early, Christians began to interpret the magi in terms of Old Testament passages such as Psalm 72:10-11: "May the kings of Tarshish and of the isles / render him tribute, / may the kings of Sheba and Seba / bring gifts. / May all kings fall down before him, / all nations give him service."

Another influential Old Testament text is Isaiah 60:3, 5-6, from which also the magi's mode of transportation is deduced: "Nations shall come to your light, / and kings to the brightness of your dawn. . . . / the wealth of the nations shall come to you. / A multitude of camels shall cover you, . . . / all those from Sheba shall come. / They shall bring gold and frankincense, / and shall proclaim the praise of the LORD."

By the sixth century, the tradition of the church had given the wise men names and identified them as kings of particular nations: Melchoir, king of Persia; Gaspar, king of India; and Balthasar, king of Arabia. Later

Imagine yourself riding a camel day after day, night after night, following a star. How would you have answered persons or even personal doubts about the wisdom of your trip? Are there ever times in your Christian journey when you hear voices telling you that it is all folly? How can you answer?

Read the quotation from Raymond Brown about "Christian midrash." (*Midrash* is an interpretive term that assumes Scripture has inexhaustible meaning and is relevant for any and every circumstance.) What interpretations have you made about the angelic, shepherd, and foreign visitors to Jesus?

Closing Prayer ■

The wise men traveled from afar and risked much to pay their homage to the Christ Child. What do you risk for your faith? Take time to make or renew your commitment to Christ.

Close with your circle prayer and include prayers for those who are discriminated against and dispossessed. Pray for God's guidance as you seek faithfulness, peace, and new life in Christ.

they were interpreted as representing the diverse races of humanity descending from the three sons of Noah—Shem, Ham, and Japheth (see Genesis 10). Nativity scenes often include figures that represent this racial diversity. While the historicity of these identifications is questionable, the theological insight is superb. The Christ Child, indeed, comes for all humankind. No racial, ethnic, or national group is excluded. All human distinctions fade into irrelevance in the light of the beckoning star of Bethlehem.

The Roman Catholic Church maintains that it still possesses relics of the original wise men. In 1162 these relics were carried from Milan to Cologne, Italy, where they were encased in a magnificent enamel shrine. In 1903, the cardinal of Cologne sent a portion of the relics back to Milan. Both cathedrals now claim such relics, which serve as a focus of pious devotion. Roman Catholic scholar Raymond Brown, writing in *The Birth of the Messiah* (Image/Doubleday, 1977), comments that "the Matthean story of the magi is a remarkable example of Christian midrash . . . . the popular and imaginative exposition of the Scriptures for faith and piety." The shepherds, the angels, the magi, the crowd of onlookers at the stable witnessed a miracle—the inbreaking of God to ordinary life in an extraordinary way—and the history of humankind has been forever altered.

"My Soul Magnifies the Lord"

Session Focus ■
We will focus on Mary's Magnificat and Simeon's Nunc Dimittis, seeking to comprehend what they communicate to us about the mission of Christ and our mission as Christ's followers.

Session Objective ■
There are two objectives for this session. First, through the canticles we can deepen our perception of how closely the New Testament gospel is linked to Old Testament roots. Second, as contemporary Christians we need to examine honestly what the coming of Christ teaches us about social, economic, and political matters.

Session Preparation ■
Read the Magnificat in Luke 1:46-55 and the Nunc Dimittis in 2:29-32 taking note of both their style and ideas. Read chapters eight through sixteen in the Book of Judith found in the Apocrypha.

Choose from among the following activities and discussion starters to plan your lesson.

Throughout Luke's infancy narrative, persons see God's power manifested and hear proclamations of the good news. In several cases, individuals who are filled with holy joy respond with outpourings of praise. We have already looked at Zechariah's *Benedictus*, spoken after the birth of his son John the Baptist (Luke 1:68-79). The *Gloria*, sung by the angel chorus, is another example (2:14). In this chapter we will consider the other two canticles in Luke—Mary's *Magnificat* (1:46-55) and Simeon's *Nunc Dimittis* (2:29-32)—and the settings in which they were uttered.

These canticles or hymns may have existed independently of Luke's narrative and then have been incorporated into it. While the words of each canticle are appropriate to the persons to whom they are attributed, there is nothing specific in them that would lose its meaning if used in another place. More than the other parts of the Gospel, the canticles are filled with echoes from the Hebrew Scriptures and Jewish intertestamental literature.

They may have originated in a Jewish Christian community called the *Anawim*. *Anawim* means "poor ones." This term probably described accurately both their economic condition and their understanding of their spiritual state. The Anawim considered themselves to be the faithful remnant of

"My Soul Magnifies the Lord" ■

Divide into clusters of three persons and share at least one time in your own life when you were so over-flowing with joy that you might have expressed your-self in a song of praise. Note the kinds of experi-ences in persons' lives that evoke such feeling.

Begin together the compo-sition of a canticle—a hymn of praise to God—stressing that the goal is not to produce great poetry. Encourage participants to take this initial group prod-uct home with them and to finish it in their own way, in their own times of prayer and devotion.

The Magnificat ■

What does it mean to understand the Magnificat as "a song of liberation"? as "a revolutionary docu-ment of intense conflict and victory"?

Read Luke 1:68-71 and 1:46-55, then read Isaiah 9:2-7. Each of these pas-sages uses lofty language to talk about what God will do and who God will send to do it. What is your emo-tional reaction to each of these celebratory announcements? How do they touch your faith? your sense of reason?

Do you see these announcements (or Mary) as paradigms (models) "of what God is doing and will

God's people. Unable to trust in their own strength, they relied upon God. The canti-cles may have been songs used in this com-munity to praise God for the sending of Jesus Christ. Luke ascribed them to his par-ticular characters in ways that remained con-sistent with their original meaning and gave voice to these characters' response to their encounters with God.

The Magnificat

The Magnificat is the great New Testament song of liberation, personal and social, moral and economic, a revolutionary document of intense conflict and victory. It praises God's liberating actions on behalf of the speaker, which are paradigmatic of all of God's actions on behalf of marginal and exploited people. We evoke the powerful memory of God's deliverance of Israel throughout its history.

The Coming of the Messiah

The Messiah, of course, was viewed as the ultimate deliverer, sent by God to turn upside down the existing world order. The majestic language Mary uses may bring to mind the powerful prophecy of Isaiah 9:6-7:

"For a child has been born for us, / a son given to us; / authority rests upon his shoulders; / and he is named / Wonderful Counselor, / Mighty God / Everlasting Father, Prince of Peace. / His authority shall grow continually / and there shall be endless peace / for the throne of David and his kingdom."

The title "Magnificat" comes from the Latin translation of its opening words; used in this context, the word *magnifies* connotes

do for exploited, impoverished, and powerless peo-
ple of all times and
places"? Explain.

the greatness of God that the speaker praises.
In Luke 1:46-49, Mary speaks of herself in
the first person. There are echoes here of
Gabriel's words to her in verses 28-30. Luke
presents Mary as the first Christian disciple.
She has accepted God's role for her (verse
38) and now is God's spokeswoman proclaiming revolution and salvation. The canticle is both an individual and a communal
song of faith and rejoicing in God. What
God has done for Mary is a paradigm of
what God is doing and will do for exploited,
impoverished, and powerless people of all
times and places.

Hannah's Song for Others

Hannah's Song for Others

Read and discuss Hannah's
song in 1 Samuel 2:1-10.
How does this compare to
Mary's Magnificat in terms
of wording, style, intent,
and content?

It is possible that Hannah's
song was an ancient hymn
of praise either that she
used or that the Bible com-
piler attributed to her,
rather than being a hymn
that she composed herself.
Does that possibility trouble you? Explain.

Consider all these words of
praise to God for what God
has done. One obvious
message is that God is
intimately involved in the
day-to-day affairs of
humankind. What other
messages do these words
convey to you?

The obvious prototype for the Magnificat
is Hannah's song in 1 Samuel 2:1-10.
Hannah praised God for the gift of a child as
she left that child at the Temple at Shiloh to
serve the Lord. Like Mary, Hannah sang of
far more than her personal situation. She
proclaimed God's mighty acts of salvation
past, present, and future.

In the Apocrypha is the stirring Book of
Judith, written in the second century B.C.
This intertestamental account includes
Judith's song of praise after she has saved her
people by beheading the general of the
invading Assyrian army. Its themes resonate
in the Magnificat.

In Luke 1:48 we hear the words of Leah, a
wife of Jacob, in Genesis 29:32 and 30:13.
Indeed, the canticle might be likened to a
quilt made of pieces assembled from the
Hebrew Scriptures and Jewish intertestamental writings.

The Magnificat proclaims that God has in
the past intervened to save God's people—
the long story of salvation history continues.
The covenant promises made to Abraham

and to David are being fulfilled. God's supreme act on behalf of the people of God is the sending of Jesus Christ. Through him, the oppressive political and economic structures will be overthrown, and a new era of justice and prosperity will take their place. The use of verbs in the past tense is not an indication that all the divine purpose has yet been accomplished. Instead, it affirms certainty and confidence about what God is doing and will do.

A Call for Justice ■

It is important to recall that, without exception, the Jewish persons who participated in the infancy narratives were among the poor and lowly of their society. They were part of a traditional agrarian society of peasants, living in rural areas and in small villages, which was being threatened. The ruinous taxes and other burdens imposed by the government during the reign of Herod caused many peasants to go deeply into debt and eventually to lose their land. Banditry became rampant as many were forced into illicit ways of making a living.

Against this background, the Magnificat can be viewed as a call for social, economic, and political justice. As such, it foreshadows later themes of Jesus' ministry. In Luke 4:16-21, Jesus proclaimed his calling: "The Spirit of the Lord is upon me, / because he has anointed me to bring good news to the poor. / He has sent me to proclaim release to the captives / and recovery of sight to the blind, / to let the oppressed go free, / to proclaim the year of the Lord's favor."

A number of Jesus' parables can best be understood by recognizing the harsh conditions of life for the common people. Jesus' gospel of radical inclusiveness, reversal of

A Call for Justice

The theme of God's judgment upon social, economic, and political injustice runs throughout the writings of the Old Testament prophets and is powerfully expressed in the life and teachings of Jesus. Consider such passages as Isaiah 1:11-17; Jeremiah 22:13-17; Amos 2:4-8 and 5:10-15, 21-24; and Micah 6:6-8. What do they tell us about the community to whom these words were addressed? What message should we derive today? What teachings, parables, and actions of Jesus that emphasize this theme do you recall? In what practical ways can (or do) you implement these injunctions to righteousness?

When you read Scripture, do you dig far enough to understand the context of the people to whom it was written? How do you reflect on the lifestyle and values of the persons for whom the text was originally intended? When you understand the context, what happens to your application of the Scripture in your own life?

Read the text box about the Pharisees. What do you remember about the Pharisees in the biblical narrative and about how Jesus deals with the Pharisees? Do you ever relate to them in one of these biblical anecdotes? Explain.

Bible 301 ☐

Use a Bible concordance to look up Pharisee, *then read several of the passages. What are the Pharisees doing in the passage? How do they intend to relate to Jesus (or to whomever)? How does Jesus respond to them? What issue is at stake, and what do you learn from the interchange?*

Then look up Pharisee *in a Bible dictionary to learn more about their respectable and faithful roots. What contrasts do you see? How can they be instructive for you?*

values, and liberation from bondage, both physical and spiritual, is the fulfillment of his mother's song of praise.

Most contemporary Christians in the United States read the Bible through a focusing lens that enables us to render it congenial, comfortable, and affirming. We consistently identify with aspects of the biblical message that we have selected carefully, if unconsciously. An example is our response to the interactions between Jesus and the Pharisees.

The Pharisees

The Pharisees are often portrayed as the "bad guys" because Jesus was very critical of their shortcomings. The Pharisees most likely had their roots in the very faithful Hasidim, who fought valiantly and died in the fight for religious freedom from Rome. At their worst portrayal in the Gospels, some Pharisees had apparently become more concerned about the "jot and tittle" of the law than the life-giving purpose and spirit of the law. When we put rules and regulations ahead of needs and compassion, we have joined the core of Pharisees whom Jesus condemned.

We tend to identify with Jesus as he points out the superficiality of their understanding of true religion. And yet, it does not take much honest thought to realize that in our day, it is we who are frequently the Pharisees. We are the morally upright, the church-going people, often the self-righteous ones. We are the respected leaders of the religious establishment of our time.

Similarly, we read Mary's powerful proclamation in the Magnificat and feel our hearts

Should middle- and upper-class, church-going Americans hear the Magnificat as good news? If not, for whom is it good news? Do you want the "proud to be scattered, the powerful brought down, and the rich sent away empty"? How, in this context, do you define "the proud," "the powerful," and "the rich"? Is that ever you?

soar with praise for the mighty work of God. But, is the good news proclaimed here really good news for us? Do we truly want the proud to be scattered, the powerful brought down, "the rich sent away empty"?

The uncomfortable truth is that for most readers of this book the Magnificat is not good news at all. It is a revolutionary document, and revolutions mean turnover in the power structure. For those of us who are on or near the top of this structure, change is not a promise but a threat. Few of us can claim to be among the lowly who will be uplifted, the hungry who will be filled. It is not we who the God of the Magnificat champions, and we will forever be unable to respond to God rightly if we do not acknowledge it.

For most of us, the Magnificat is only understood authentically when it is recognized as a proclamation of judgment. We truly hear its message only if we repent and allow the Holy Spirit to teach us what it means to be poor and lowly.

The Consecration of Jesus

On the eighth day of the infant Jesus' life, he was circumcised (Luke 2:21) and named. Circumcision has been the sign of the covenant between God and the Hebrew people since the time of Abraham (Genesis 17:9-14). By circumcision Jesus became a part of the community in covenant with God. He also was given officially the name decreed by Gabriel at the Annunciation to Mary. "Jesus" is a shortened form of "Joshua," and it was a very popular name of the time. The name remained common among the Jews until the early second century when its Christian connotation caused it to be avoided.

Luke continues to emphasize the theme of

The Consecration of Jesus

Divide into four groups and have each look briefly at portions of the Old Testament laws upon which the events related in Luke 2:21-24 are based—Genesis 17:9-14; Exodus 12:21-32 and 13:1-2, 11-16; Leviticus 12; and Numbers 18:15-16. Note the parallels and differences between circumcision as the sign of the covenant between God and the Jewish people and baptism as the sign of the covenant between God and the Christian church.

obedience to the law. Some weeks later, Jesus' parents took him to the Temple for what the church has traditionally called the Presentation, celebrated on February 2. In Luke 2:22-24, Luke's unfamiliarity with the details of Jewish practice appears to have caused him to confuse the ceremonies described.

Presentation or consecration of the child to God was required by the law in Exodus 13:1-2, "The LORD said to Moses: 'Consecrate to me all the firstborn; whatever is the first to open the womb among the Israelites, of human beings and animals, is mine.' " This consecration was a reminder of the power of God who had brought the Israelites out of bondage in Egypt. It commemorated especially the sparing of the Hebrew first-born when God sent a plague of death upon the Egyptians, as indicated in Exodus 13:11-16. (See also Exodus 12:21-32.)

Originally this was probably interpreted as requiring that the first-born would be given for service in the tabernacle or Temple. We have already mentioned this in the case of Samuel, the son of Hannah. As noted in Numbers 18:15-16, the first-born could be "redeemed" or bought back from this service. This provision was possible because the Levites were made responsible for worship life in the holy places. The redemption price of five shekels was to be paid at the Temple. As the account is written in Luke 2:22-24, Jesus was not redeemed from his consecration and service to God.

What are the current rituals in which we participate to "consecrate" our children? What are the similarities in the symbolism, if not the ritual, with the celebratory customs that we use today and those observed by Joseph and Mary with Jesus?

Review Luke 1–2 to determine how many occasions Luke tells us (or implies) that some event occurred to fulfill the word of God or that the persons involved took care to follow the law. What do these references tell you about the intentions of God in the affairs of humanity and about the intentions of faithful persons to devote themselves to the affairs of God?

What do you do that fulfills the law of the Lord?

Bible 301 ☐

Using a Bible dictionary, research redemption and the significance of the first-born. How did Mary and Joseph fulfill the law? What might it have meant

The First-born

The role of the first-born male child was a very important one in the Hebrew society, although their history is full of examples of reversals in which a later-born son takes prece-

dence. *The first-born son became the head of the household or clan when his father died, and the son received a double share of the inheritance. One of many exceptions to this custom was with Judah, the fourth son of Jacob (Israel), who rises to prominence in the text of Genesis. Judah is the son through whom the lineage of Jesus is traced back to Abraham (Matthew 1:2-3); and it is in connection with Judah that Tamar, one of several women in the genealogy, is also mentioned.*

The Purification ■
Read Leviticus 12:1-8 and Luke 2:22-24. A woman during a time of "impurity" could not visit the Temple (at least half the time during childbearing years), because of her monthly cycle (two weeks a month) and the added time after childbirth. Given these restrictions, how might Mary have felt upon attending to a required ritual at the Temple? How would you feel today about such exclusion (if you are a woman) or about having women in your life excluded?

Note the sacrifices offered. They suggest that Jesus' family was poor. Many of our churches need a fairly affluent congregation in order to pay for the mortgage and upkeep of the church and the salary and benefits of the pastor, not to mention the cost of ministry and outreach. Do you think the church would benefit from having clear (and enforceable) expectations about gifts

The Purification

The other ceremony, which Luke has blended with the consecration and redemption, is that of purification. The law as stipulated in Leviticus 12 required this. "If a woman conceives and bears a male child, she shall be ceremonially unclean seven days (Leviticus 12:2). . . . Her time of blood purification shall be thirty-three days" (verse 4). (Incidentally, these times were doubled in the case of a female child.)

At the end of this time period—forty days—an offering was to be brought to the priest who "shall make atonement on her behalf, and she shall be clean" (verse 8). If the woman's family could not afford to offer a sheep, pigeons could be substituted. Like the animals, birds for this purpose were sold in the Temple court. The poverty of Jesus' family is revealed by their giving of sacrificial birds.

Clearly Luke has combined these distinct rituals into one, either out of ignorance or for literary purposes. Another peculiar note is the reference to "their purification" in Luke 2:22. There was no requirement or practice of purification for the father. The account serves well for Luke's purpose of

to the church on the basis of ability to pay? Explain.

Simeon ■

Review Luke 2:25-35. Note where the Scripture states or implies the work of the Holy Spirit. How does God work with Simeon? How does his character and experience compare with Zechariah's in Luke 1?

Imagine that you are like Simeon, waiting in faithful expectation for something you are sure God has promised. What might it be? Are you waiting for something specific? How do you think you would recognize this event (or whatever you expected) when it finally arrived?

Sometimes what we seek is in front of us, and we don't see it because we're busy looking in all the wrong places. How do you deal with this danger, especially regarding God's plans?

Mary, Joseph, and the others in this Gospel infancy narrative seem to have some specific direction (to fulfill the law or to receive or act on a well-timed word from an angel, for example) that guides them in their expectations regarding God's plans. What signs do you feel, experience, or see? How do you know these are signs? How do you find clarity in

getting the family to the Temple in Jerusalem where they will meet Simeon and Anna.

Simeon

Luke 2:25-35 relates the story of Simeon's interaction with the infant Jesus and his family. The meeting was at the Temple; it must have been in either the Court of Gentiles or the Court of Women, in order for Mary to have been there. Simeon is introduced as a good and pious man. He was waiting for the coming of the Messiah and believed that God had promised that he would not die until he had seen it happen. He might also be considered a prophet. Three times in verses 25-27 Simeon is said to be in close communication with the Holy Spirit.

The scene in the Temple must have been deeply moving. After years of waiting and yearning, Simeon's faith was rewarded. He saw before him the infant whom, through the revelation of the Holy Spirit, he knew to be the Messiah. When Simeon took the child into his arms, the old man burst forth with a canticle of praise. It is traditionally called the *Nunc Dimittis* from the first words of the Latin translation. Simeon spoke of himself as a slave who was being emancipated, now that he had seen the Messiah. He declared that this child is "your [God's] salvation" available to "all peoples." Israel's God has granted salvation to both Jews and Gentiles. This is highly significant to Luke as can be seen in his "second volume," the Book of Acts, with its theme of spreading the gospel to the Gentiles.

The Nunc Dimittis may have been used on occasions of the deaths of early Christians. Certainly it is an appropriate statement of the attitude with which

knowing what your life work or goals may be, as Simeon seems to have done?

Review Luke 2:33-35, Simeon's second word or his prophecy of the "sword." What does he mean? We have the benefit of twenty centuries of hindsight, but how might Mary and Joseph have interpreted this statement? How do these words reveal Jesus' role in God's salvation history?

Christians of that day and this can face death: "Master, now you are dismissing your servant in peace, / according to your word; / for my eyes have seen your salvation . . ." (Luke 2:29-30). Since the fifth century, the Nunc Dimittis has been a part of the monastic Office of the Hours, being recited in the night prayers of the church. Certainly Simeon is a forceful reminder of the reality at the heart of life for us all. It is only after we have embraced Christ that we are ready to die.

Simeon's words to Mary in verses 33-35 interject a note of sadness in the face of rejoicing. Some in Israel will accept God's salvation in Christ, but others will reject it. Mary herself will accept, but not without trial and pain. The "sword [that] will pierce" Mary's own soul will starkly reveal what is in each person's inmost being (Luke 2:35; see also 12:1-2). Perhaps there is here also a hint of the suffering that Mary will experience decades later as her son is crucified.

Bible 301 ☐

Read the information about widows in the box on "Righteous Widows" and look up the specific references. Then look up widow in a Bible dictionary for more information on the status and situation of the widow in this biblical era. Keep this in mind as you study Anna.

Righteous Widows

Luke is interested in the contributions women make to Jesus' personal story and ministry, as evident in the inclusion of the story about Anna. In addition to the women who are healed, who contribute to his ministry, and who host Jesus in their home, Luke speaks several times about righteous widows.

The next after Anna is the widow at Sidon with whom Elijah resided and cared for during a famine (1 Kings 17:1-16). Jesus mentioned the story (Luke 4:24-26) to point out that even poor foreigners could and would respond to his message.

Luke then reports the healing of the son of a widow at Nain (7:11-17) and likens the pleas for justice of the poor to a poor widow who relentlessly brought her complaint to a judge (18:1-8). The judge eventually had to respond to her. In the same vein, Jesus criticized the scribes who "devour widow's houses" (20:45-47).

The last righteous widow mentioned in Luke is the woman whom Jesus observed in the Temple treasury. Seeing that she contributed little in substance but greatly in sacrifice, Jesus praised her generosity and used it as an object lesson in the uncharitable giving of the wealthy (21:1-4).

Anna

Continuing the pattern of pairing that characterizes Luke's Gospel, he next introduces a woman, Anna. She is the only woman in the New Testament to be called a prophet. Anna was an old woman who, like Simeon, had lived for years in great piety and prayer, waiting for the coming of Christ. The emphasis on the length of her widowhood points to the special role of widows in the early Christian community, as mentioned in Acts and the epistles. There are six additional references in Luke's Gospel to pious widows. Like Simeon, Anna broke forth in praise to God. She also "preached"—proclaiming the good news of Christ (verse 38).

Return to Nazareth

After observing the rituals and meeting with Simeon and Anna, Jesus' family returned to their hometown of Nazareth. There, "the child grew and became strong, filled with wisdom; and the favor of God was upon him" (verse 40). This description is much like that of the boy Samuel in 1 Samuel 2:26 and that of the young John the Baptist in Luke 1:80. Once again, Luke's

Anna ■

Note the emphasis upon Anna's widowhood in Luke 2:36-38. How does what you know about biblical-era widows affect your insight into Anna's place in Jesus' story? What did she do? What, in that society, did it mean for a woman to prophesy?

In many churches today, widows comprise a large percentage of the congregation. What are some of the implications of this fact? What are the needs and opportunities?

Return to Nazareth ■

Compare the references to these "growing boys." The Holy Family returned at that point to the routine of daily life. Do you find holy activity in your regular routine? Where do you see God at work to help you "grow strong in faith and favor with the Lord"?

Closing Prayer ■

Simeon and Anna waited with great expectation for the Savior and Redeemer, and they devoted their lives to God's service while they waited. Take time in prayer to review your commitment to God and then to make or renew your covenant.

Close with your circle prayer, including prayers for justice for all God's people and for insight as to your own responsibility in the face of so much injustice.

story of Jesus Christ is linked to the Old Testament story of Israel's salvation history, with the Baptist serving as a bridge between them.

Session Eight

The Child, His Birth

Session Focus ■

In this concluding session, we seek to discover what factual information exists and what we can responsibly assume about Jesus' early years.

Session Objective ■

There are two major objectives for this session. One is to foster increased appreciation of Jesus as a human being by describing the setting in which his early life was lived. Second, the session attempts to emphasize the amazing act of God who became one of us in the person of Jesus.

Session Preparation ■

Check your church or local library for books that include biblical art. If you can, obtain a copy of *The Lost Books of the Bible,* which includes the Protevangelion, and the other infancy narratives. Have on hand a Bible dictionary and Bible atlas.

After all of our discussion of the historical setting, characters, and events associated with the coming of Christ, it is somewhat surprising to note how little we are told about the birth itself. The first chapter of Matthew ends with the assertion that Joseph, informed by the angel of the unusual circumstances of Mary's pregnancy, married her but had no sexual relations with her until after the birth. From this point, Matthew leaps immediately to the story of the wise men, leaving the reader to ascertain that the birth had occurred sometime in between. Nothing is said about the time or place.

Luke offers a bit more detail. He places the birth in Bethlehem in some place other than the overcrowded inn. Church tradition very early began to speak of the location of the birth as a cave. Caves were often used as stables for sheltering animals. In the early fourth century, the Emperor Constantine had a basilica built over several caves in Bethlehem.

Luke specifies that Mary wrapped her child "in bands of cloth"—"swaddling clothes" in the King James Version; "swaddling clothes" in the Revised Standard Version—"and laid him in a manger." Such wrapping was the common way that a responsible mother attended to her newborn. Luke mentions it twice, in 2:7 and 12. His point may be that, despite the impoverished

Choose from among these
activities and discussion
starters to plan your
lesson.

His Birth ■

Recall living Nativity
scenes or Christmas
pageants in which you, or
perhaps your children or
grandchildren, participated.
What is the emotional
response to being a part of
such a presentation? How
effective are these presen-
tations in communicating
the truth of the Christian
gospel?

His Identity
and Mission ■

Read Luke 2:41-52.
Imagine yourself as one of
the frantic parents looking
for the twelve-year-old
Jesus. How would you
behave when you finally
found him in the Temple?
Discuss Mary and Joseph's
reaction to what Jesus did
and said.

What would Jesus and the
teachers have been talking
about? Note Luke 4:32
and 20:26. What does
Jesus mean by his reply to
his parents' question?
What does Jesus see as his
mission in life?

circumstances of his birth, this child was
received and cared for, not neglected or
unwanted.

In Ezekiel 16:4, Jerusalem is metaphori-
cally described as an outcast child who was
"[not] wrapped in cloths." The manger in
which the child is laid is mentioned three
times, in Luke 2:7, 12, and 16. A manger was
a trough for feeding animals and indicates
the impoverished circumstances in which the
birth occurred. Animals were added to the
imagined birth scene over time, probably
because of the manger and the idea of there
being a stable.

Christian art over the centuries has elabo-
rated on the scene. An intriguing twentieth-
century portrayal is the painting by Italian-
American Joseph Stella entitled *The Creche*.
The use of figures arranged into Nativity
scenes or creches was popularized by Saint
Francis of Assisi who began the custom in a
midnight Mass in 1223.

Claiming His Identity and Mission

Luke 2:41-52 provides the only glimpse
that we have in the New Testament of the
time between the events associated with
Jesus' birth and the beginning of his public
ministry. Matthew leaps immediately from an
account of the family's return from Egypt to
the public ministry of John the Baptist and
Jesus' coming to him to be baptized. Mark's
Gospel begins with John the Baptist and
Jesus' baptism. After a prologue about the
pre-existence of the Christ, the Gospel of
John also moves to the ministry of the
Baptist.

As Luke repeatedly emphasizes, Joseph
and Mary were faithful Jews and obedient to
the law. This obedience to the law included
journeying to Jerusalem at least once a year

Mary and Joseph did not understand what Jesus said to them. Think about a time when you struggled to understand someone else's motivations for worrisome behavior, especially a child's. What did you do? How did the issue finally resolve itself? Did your faith in God influence what happened? If so, how?

Bible 301 ☐

Discuss Stella's The Creche *or any other paintings of the scene that are available. What do you find striking? surprising?*

History's Record ■

Why do you think there is so little historical (non-biblical) reference to Jesus? The few existing references generally look at Jesus in the context of being the instigator in a nuisance sect. Try to imagine that you do not have the benefit of two thousand years of history. Does it seem surprising that outsiders saw early Christianity as a sect and

for the Festival of Passover. An individual could complete the trip in three days, but it probably took four to five days with a group of families. Two days had likely passed by the time Jesus' parents became aware that he was not with the group and returned to Jerusalem to find him.

The account of his conversations with the teachers is not implausible. Jewish boys learned the law and Israel's salvation history from their elders. Jesus was clearly a precocious child. The teachers' reaction of amazement was like that of others who later heard Jesus teach. (See Luke 4:32 and 20:26.) The point of this story of an incident during Jesus' youth is not so much to stress his precocity as it is to contrast his understanding of himself to that of his parents. In 2:49, Jesus looked ahead and announced that he understood his life mission. He claimed for himself a special relationship with God. In this vignette Luke reminds his readers that Jesus was the Son of God from his conception in Mary's womb and throughout his maturing years. His parents, in spite of the dramatic events surrounding his birth, were still unclear about how his divine sonship would be lived out.

History's Record

Other than this episode in the Temple at age twelve, we know nothing about Jesus' life until the beginning of his public ministry when he was about thirty years old. This may be an appropriate point to interject some information about our knowledge of Jesus in general. Basically what we know is what the New Testament tells us and almost all of that is found in the Gospels.

There is little historical information in other sources. The Jewish historian Josephus

Christians as a bunch of troublemakers? Explain.

mentions Jesus twice in his *Antiquities of the Jews* written around A.D. 93. One of these is in a reference to the execution of James who is identified as "the brother of Jesus who is called Messiah." The other passage has been edited by Christian writers, but provides additional evidence that Josephus knew of the existence of Jesus.

Historical Christianity

Suetonius, a Roman writer, was probably one of the first non-Christian writers to mention Christianity. In a somewhat garbled account in his writing, Lives of the Caesars, Suetonius mentioned the expulsion of Jews from Rome because they had caused a disturbance "at the instigation of Chrestus," understood to mean Jesus Christ.

Discuss the John Meier quotation about Jesus' "marginality." Is this a disparaging assessment, or is it a helpful insight into who Jesus was?

Three Roman historians—Pliny, Suetonius, and Tacitus—mention Jesus and the early-Christian community. Jewish rabbis of the first and second centuries refer to Jesus infrequently and in ways that discredit him, although they do not deny his ministry. Scholar John Meier (*A Marginal Jew*, Anchor Bible Reference Library; Doubleday, 1991) helps put this in perspective: "This simply reminds us that Jesus was a marginal Jew leading a marginal movement in a marginal province of a vast Roman Empire. The wonder is that any learned Jew or pagan would have known or referred to him at all in the first and early second century."

The "Hidden Years" ■

Read the two excerpts from the infancy narratives set apart from the main text, pages 103–05. How do

The "Hidden Years"

The other set of sources for information about Jesus is the apocryphal gospels. These are books about Jesus written by early

you react to the stories about Jesus in these apocryphal gospels? Does this material have any value in helping us to know him better?

In Thomas's infancy gospel, which was written about a century after Jesus died, Jesus is portrayed as mean and vindictive. What purpose could it serve the early church to believe that as a child Jesus behaved in such a way?

Christians, which were not accepted into the New Testament canon. At least two of these books are classified as infancy gospels because they tell of Jesus' birth and childhood. *The Infancy Gospel of Thomas* was probably written about A.D. 150 in an attempt to fill the gap left by Luke between Jesus' birth and his twelfth year. It "presents the child Jesus as a self-willed little brat" who kills off playmates when they anger him, a "sinister superboy [who] belongs more in a horror movie than a gospel," writes Meier.

Thomas's Gospel of the Infancy

It is not difficult to understand why Thomas's Gospel was not accepted into the canon. The young Jesus is portrayed as mean and vindictive. Consider this incident.

"Another time Jesus went forth into the street, and a boy running by, rushed upon his shoulder; At which Jesus being angry, said to him, thou shalt go no farther. And he instantly fell down dead: Which when some persons saw, they said, Where was this boy born, that everything which he says presently cometh to pass? Then the parents of the dead boy going to Joseph complained, saying, You are not fit to live with us, in our city, having such a boy as that: Either teach him that he bless and not curse, or else depart hence with him, for he kills our children" (2:7-12).

Joseph attempted to correct him, but Jesus struck blind those who had accused him. When Joseph cuffed his ear, Jesus warned his father to watch out. "Trouble me no more" (2:20).

The second is entitled *The Protoevangelion of James*. It too was probably written in the second century and for the same purpose. It

In a similar way, legends have developed around various persons in the history of our nation. George Washington, Abraham Lincoln, and Daniel Boone are examples. Share some of these stories. Why do such legends develop? What do they tell us about the person?

What are the values of our "educated guesses" and speculations about aspects of the life of Jesus that are not dealt with in the Bible? What, if any, are the dangers involved?

In the other infancy narrative, Jesus and Judas Iscariot had an encounter. Does the later story of the betrayal take on any added significance if we believe that Satan had entered Judas even as a child? (See Luke 22:3-4.) Does it take on added significance if we think that Jesus had healed Judas of an evil spirit and then was later betrayed by him?

Bible 301 ☐

If you have access to the complete copy, read more in these infancy narratives. What else do they say about Jesus' family life and relationship with his parents? about how Mary and Joseph cared for him? What light, if any, can these stories shed on Jesus and how the early Christian church thought about him?

opens with the story of Mary's parents, continues with a jumbling of the Matthew and Luke infancy narratives, and ends with the slaying of Zechariah by officers of Herod. These narratives make entertaining, often amusing, reading, but they add little if anything to our knowledge of the "hidden years" of Jesus' life.

Numerous legends about Jesus appear in a wide variety of writings from the early centuries of Christianity. There are accounts of a trip taken to India and of contact with Buddhist teachers in Alexandria, Egypt. Other stories feature Jesus as an apprentice to magicians in Egypt, learning their craft to be used in his ministry. Various possibilities of a relationship with the Qumran communities are suggested.

The fact is that we have no need of any of these exotic influences to explain Jesus. Everything known about him can be well accounted for by the Jewish tradition itself. Regrettably, there are no historically reliable stories about Jesus before the beginning of his public ministry at age thirty.

The First Gospel of the Infancy

The First Gospel of the Infancy of Jesus Christ shows Jesus in a more kindly light, although this writing is not accepted as part of the canon. In this gospel, young Judas Iscariot was a neighbor of Jesus, but he was "seized by Satan." Jesus, even as a toddler, could work miracles.

"But the mother of this miserable boy, hearing of St. Mary and her son Jesus, arose presently, and taking her son in her arms, brought him to the Lady Mary. In the meantime, James and Joses had taken away the infant, the Lord Jesus, to play at a proper season with other children. . . . Then Judas, who was possessed, came and sat

down at the right hand of Jesus. When Satan was acting upon him as usual, he went about to bite the Lord Jesus. And because he could not do it, he struck Jesus on the right side, so that he cried out. And in the same moment Satan went out of the boy, and ran away like a mad dog" (14:3-8).

The Village of Nazareth

The Village of Nazareth

Locate a map of Palestine, preferably in a Bible atlas, but one in your Bible will do. Find the four major geographic regions and note various areas, towns, and bodies of water that are familiar from your Bible study.

In the atlas or a Bible dictionary, look up *Nazareth* and *Sepphoris*. What added information did you find that help fix the context of Jesus' life and early years?

If you have been to the Holy Land, recall the indigenous food you ate. (Breakfast especially, with choices such as fish, raw tomatoes, and cucumbers, for example, may seem strange to the US palate.) What about spices, seasonings, and condiments? Were these foods similar to what the Israelites would have had in the first century? Did you have any feelings about eating the same kinds of foods Jesus must have eaten?

Let us sketch the early years of Jesus' life as fully and accurately as possible. He grew up in the village of Nazareth—a place never mentioned in the Old Testament. Nazareth was located in Galilee in the central highlands area of Palestine. While these mountains are not high, they stand in contrast to the narrow coastal strip bordering the Mediterranean Sea—the land of the Philistine enemies in the Old Testament. From Galilee one can see the Mediterranean less than twenty miles away.

In the southern part of these central highlands, Jerusalem is built on a mountain. East of the city, through Jericho and on to the Dead Sea, is the desolate Wilderness of Judea where Jesus after his baptism was tempted by the devil. West of the central highlands is the Jordan Valley, through which the river runs from the Sea of Galilee to the Dead Sea. Parts of the valley were a thick jungle with dangerous animals such as bears and lions. Between the Jordan Valley and the Arabian Desert is a large plateau known as the eastern tableland.

Nazareth is less than four miles from Sepphoris, the largest city in Galilee. Sepphoris was destroyed by the Roman forces putting down the revolt that broke out at Herod's death in 4 B.C. During Jesus' boyhood it was rebuilt as a rather cosmopolitan

Note the information about the economy and think about the parables you know. How do they make use of images, ideas, and "facts of life" that would have been familiar to Jesus' hearers? If Jesus came to your hometown, what images might he use in the parables he told you?

city. Four other cities were located within four miles of Nazareth; we should not think of the village as provincial or isolated.

The economy of Jesus' home area was largely agricultural. While the soil was fairly fertile in some parts, it was often rocky and required hard work. Major crops included wheat and barley, grapes (used chiefly for wine) from the vineyards, and olive trees with their fruit as the source of oil for cooking and other purposes. Pomegranates and figs were common. Livestock was also important. Goats produced milk and black hair used for making tents. Sheep provided wool, milk, and meat. The importance of agriculture is evidenced by the three chief Jewish festivals, all of which were related to the harvest. The people fished in the Sea of Galilee—really a small lake—which was deep and filled with an abundance of fish.

Life at Home

Look up *education* in a Bible dictionary. Then read Mark 6:1-3 in which Jesus astonishes his hearers with his insight, and quite possibly incurs their ridicule for "stepping above his class." If males typically were taught the law and were expected to speak from time to time in the synagogue, why do you think Jesus would have so surprised his hearers?

Life at Home

What then can we responsibly surmise about the "hidden years" of Jesus' life? Certainly he grew up in a devout Jewish home where he was taught the Hebrew Scriptures and participated in the festivals and holy days of Judaism. He would have been educated at home, or possibly in the synagogue, where his education would have emphasized reading and writing Torah. Because of the great reverence for Torah and the passion for its study, literacy was very important for Jewish men. He would have learned biblical Hebrew and have been able to use it in his later debates with the scribes and Pharisees. The everyday language that Jesus spoke would have been Aramaic, the common tongue of Jewish peasants. In addition, he probably knew and used some common Greek, since it was the language of trade

We identify Jesus as a carpenter (see Mark 6:3) who was taught the trade by his father (see Matthew 13:55). Learned men did not pursue carpentry, which suggests an humble trade and lifestyle. Yet Jesus was a wonderful teacher. Does it seem strange that a "blue collar worker" could have such gifts? Have you ever been surprised when someone you expected to have only a particular level of education or insight revealed a deeper intelligence than you had imagined? What was that experience like? Did prejudice play a part in your expectations?

Despite the importance that Jewish society of that day placed on marriage and children, as far as we know, Jesus never married. Why might he have made such a decision? Do you think that his choice has any relevance for us today? Is his apparent singleness justification for requiring clergy persons to be unmarried? Explain. (Peter and, no doubt, many or most of the disciples were married; so clearly married disciples did not trouble Jesus.)

and used for communication with Gentiles. No evidence indicates that he knew Latin.

His family was of the artisan class—below agrarian peasants in the social order, although if they were not completely landless, they may have done some farming for subsistence. Jesus is identified as a carpenter only in Mark 6:3a. Probably this term is better understood as woodworker. Due to the scarcity of trees, few buildings in Palestine were made of wood. He and Joseph probably made wood products such as doors, frames, roof beams, furniture, cabinets, chests, plows, and yokes. This trade required physical strength and technical skill.

As a child in Nazareth, Jesus may have played games similar to hopscotch and jacks. Archaeological discoveries have yielded toys including whistles, tops, rattles, and toy animals on wheels. He and his family would have eaten two meals daily. Breakfast was typically eaten at midmorning, having been carried to work. Flat bread, cheese, and olives were staples. On the dinner menu might be vegetable stew, fruit, eggs, perhaps fish, and even locusts, along with the usual bread and cheese. Jesus was apparently never married, something that his society would have expected him to do by his early twenties. This was an unusual decision for a Jewish man of the day. Jews celebrated sexuality, marriage, and procreation as good gifts from God. Jesus presumably understood his God-given mission to require sacrifice of the customary experiences of marriage and family. There is perhaps a hint of this in Matthew 19:12 when Jesus speaks of eunuchs, including those "who have made themselves eunuchs for the kingdom of heaven," a metaphor for celibacy.

We must remember that all of this information is speculative, based simply upon what we know of the lives of Jewish people in the first century. It remains true that we simply have little factual knowledge about Jesus' life before he was baptized and began his public ministry.

The Scandal ■

Have you ever thought about Christianity as a "scandal" or a "scandal of particularity"? What might those who lived in Jesus' day and were exposed to his ministry and his claims have regarded as scandalous? Discuss and analyze this remark: "The hinge of history is attached to a stable door in Bethlehem."

What is it about Christianity that makes one a Christian? Divide into two teams and debate the pros and cons of this statement: "Only persons who accept Jesus Christ as Savior and Lord can go to heaven." (One does not necessarily have to be convinced of the truth of a position in order to debate it this way.)

The Scandal

Christianity is a scandalous faith. In a variety of ways, it violates our commonly accepted standards of knowledge and truth. How could a Jewish child born in disreputable circumstances in a far way place at a long ago time have any significance for our lives here and now? The shocking thing about Christianity is its claim that the coming of the Christ Child transformed the world and the lives of human beings in it. As someone has said, "The hinge of history is attached to a stable door in Bethlehem."

Opinion polls give evidence that almost all persons in this nation believe in the existence of God. Overwhelming majorities believe that God knows and cares about them. Most say that they try to lead good moral lives. Many even claim to pray daily. Is this Christianity? The disturbing, uncomfortable answer is "no."

Although it may appear to be narrow, even arrogant, the Christian faith makes very specific assertions about God and the relationship between God and us. This means that Christianity is grounded on the scandal of particularity. We believe that out of all the multitudes of people on the earth, God, for God's own reasons, chose the descendants of Abraham. God chose a particular people—the Jews—as the people through whose history God would work at the task of restoring sinful humanity to the loving relationship

Closing Prayer

Jesus came from humble beginnings and, by worldly standards, died in even more lowly circumstances; yet Jesus' life had, and continues to have, a tremendous impact in the world. That humility and ordinariness affirms that anyone can have a life devoted to God and that God values and has a good use for that life. Take time in prayer to make or reaffirm your commitment to Jesus Christ.

with God that we were created to enjoy.

We believe that God got even more specific and, quite literally, "down to earth." God chose a particular time, a particular place, a particular family, and a particular individual. In Jesus of Nazareth "all the fullness of God was pleased to dwell" (Colossians 1:19). In a way that far exceeds our understanding, Jesus was both totally human and totally divine.

The doctrine of Incarnation teaches that in Jesus, God is with us; God is among us; God is one of us. When we seek to know what God is like, we look to Jesus. When we seek to know what kind of people we should be, we look to Jesus. All that we need to know, all that we can know, all that the human mind can grasp about divinity is revealed in Jesus Christ.

This scandal of particularity does not mean that all other religions are wrong or false. God can be made known to any degree God wishes in any and all religions. Persons of other faiths are seeking the same God as are Christians—there is, after all, only one. We cannot necessarily know how God relates to persons of other faiths. We can and do know that divine love has no limits. Christianity is bold enough to say that other religions are "going about it the hard way." It is in Jesus Christ that God is most fully revealed and is most directly accessible.